THE OFFICIAL

CONSUMERS GUIDE TO HYPNOTISM

Edited By

DR. DWIGHT DAMON

President - National Guild of Hypnotists, Inc.

The World's Oldest and Largest Hypnotism

Membership Organization

Easy-to-understand information from

Leading International Hypnotism

Authors, Columnists, & Instructors

First Edition - July 2004
Second Edition - April 2005
Third Edition - September 2008

Cover design by Melody Bachand.

ISBN Number1-885846-06-1

PO Box 308 - Merrimack, NH 03054
(603) 429-9438 Fax: (603) 424-8066
Email: ngh@ngh.net www.ngh.net

Foreword
by Ormond McGill

The Consumer Guide To Hypnotism will be found a treasure trove of information for the busy person who wants to obtain knowledge of this fascinating subject.

The book will prove of value to both professional hypnotists and the general public who daily are mounting in numbers of persons who have become interested in this continuously mounting subject of popular interest.

Edited by Dr. Dwight F. Damon, President of the prestigious National Guild of Hypnotists, Inc. The Consumer Guide covers the nitty-gritty of this fascinating subject in a nutshell format.

It is truly amazing how much pertinent information about hypnosis has been squeezed in these pages. Many answers to questions about hypnotism you may wish to know (and possibly much more) will be found in this guide.

The information is accurate, presented in fifty easy-to-understand chapters authored by fifty experts in the field. A glance at contents will be found astonishing in the extent of its coverage. Literally an entire library of hypnotic literature unfolds before you.

Ormond McGill
Palo Alto, CA
U.S.A. 2004

Contents

Chapter 1 - Introduction - Donald J. Mottin - Pg 1

Chapter 2 - What is Hypnosis? - John C. Hughes - Pg 3

Chapter 3 - How To Find A Referral - Melody Bachand - Pg 5

Chapter 4 - Your First Hypnotism Visit - Patricia MacIsaac - Pg 7

Chapter 5 - Myths & Misconceptions - Edward Morris - Pg 9

Chapter 6 - Share With Your Hypnotist - Anne Spencer - Pg 11

Chapter 7 - Hypnosis Rapid Results - Georgina Cannon - Pg 15

Chapter 8 - The Union & Hypnotism- Sharon Morris - Pg 17

Chapter 9 - Hypnotism Training - Richard Harte - Pg 19

Chapter 10 - Self-Hypnosis - Norbert Bakas - Pg 21

Chapter 11 - Weight Control & Hypnosis - Thomas Nicoli - Pg 23

Chapter 12 - Medical/Dental Hypnosis - Bill Breuer - Pg 25

Chapter 13 - Hypnosis & Dentistry - Dr. Jack Flanagan - Pg 27

Chapter 14 - Religion & Hypnotism - Rev. Lindsay Bates - Pg 29

Chapter 15 - Scientific Evidence - Madelaine Lawrence - Pg 31

Chapter 16 - Hypnotherapy vs. Psychotherapy - Gerald Kein - Pg 33

Chapter 17 - Differences of Titles - Tony DeMarco - Pg 35

Chapter 18 - Hypno-Birthing® & Hypnosis - Marie Mongan - Pg 37

Chapter 19 - Medical Hypnotism - C. Scot Giles - Pg 39

Chapter 20 - Forensic Hypnosis - George Baranowski - Pg 41

Chapter 21 - Pediatric Hypnosis - Don Rice - Pg 45

Chapter 22 - Hypnosis & Study Skills - Fiona Biddle - Pg 47

Chapter 23 - Hypnosis in Geriatrics - Maurice Kershaw - Pg 49

Chapter 24 - Smoking Cessation - Jacob Bimblich - Pg 51

Chapter 25 - Diabetes and Hypnosis - C. Devin Hastings - Pg 53

Chapter 26 - Sleep & Hypnosis - Debbie Papadakis - Pg 55

Chapter 27 - Creativity & Hypnosis - Kimble Bromley - Pg 57

Chapter 28 - Pain - Ron Eslinger - Pg 59

Chapter 29 - Sports & Hypnosis - Bob Reese - Pg 61

Chapter 30 - HypnoCoaching® - Lisa Halpin - Pg 63

Chapter 31 - Parenting & Hypnotism - Sue Fox - Pg 65

Chapter 32 - Taking Control of Fear - Cynthia Thomas - Pg 67

Chapter 33 - Entertainment & Hypnosis - Jerry Valley - Pg 69

Chapter 34 - Hypnoanalysis - Shaun Brookhouse - Pg 73

Chapter 35 - Hypnotic Age Regression - Calvin Banyan - Pg 75

Chapter 36 - Past Lives - Charlene Ackerman - Pg 77

Chapter 37 - Guided Imagery - Mary Elizabeth Raines - Pg 81

Chapter 38 - Massage & Hypnosis - Bob Adams - Pg 83

Chapter 39 - Conversational Hypnosis - Kevin Hogan - Pg 87

Chapter 40 - Subconscious Behavior Patterns - Don Mottin - Pg 89

Chapter 41 - HYPNOmotivation® - Dwight Damon & Patricia MacIsaac - Pg 91

Chapter 42 - Innovations of Hypnosis - Larry Garrett - Pg 95

Chapter 43 - Cancer & Hypnotism - C. Scot Giles - Pg 97

Chapter 44 - ESP & Hypnosis - Ramona Garcia - Pg 99

Chapter 45 - Parts Hypnosis - C. Roy Hunter - Pg 101

Chapter 46 - What is NLP? - William Horton - Pg 103

Chapter 47 - Past Life Regression - Henry Leo Bolduc - Pg 107

Chapter 48 - Dreams & Hypnotism - Bree Ferrario - Pg 109

Chapter 49 - Spirituality & Hypnotism - Marilyn Gordon - Pg 111

Chapter 50 - Light Touch - Constance Palinsky - Pg 113

National Guild of Hypnotists, Inc.
PO Box 308
Merrimack, NH 03054-0308

(603) 429-9438 Fax: (603) 424-8066
Email: ngh@ngh.net
Web site: http://www.ngh.net

Chapter 1
Introduction

You will learn a lot from this publication. We have commissioned a wide range of articles from top hypnotism professionals to help acquaint the average layperson with an almost encyclopedic source of information. We hope to answer a lot of your questions and perhaps to awaken an interest in readers who might consider training for a career in the exciting field of hypnotism.

The National Guild of Hypnotists was organized in Boston, Massachusetts late in 1950, and expanded so rapidly that it was effectively established and recognized nationwide in 1951. It is now incorporated as a not-for-profit educational membership organization with the goal of maintaining a separate and distinct profession for hypnotists. We would like to tell you a bit about the organization and the man who has been its driving force.

Dr. Dwight F. Damon, president of the National Guild of Hypnotists, has methodically built the professional practice of hypnotism into a distinct and respectable profession. He has spent half a century attracting an international membership of over 10,000 hypnotists in 65 countries. He has done so much in an unassuming way that many professional hypnotists, who are greatly in his debt, have assumed his contribution to the profession as a matter of course. Yet, the development of the profession was by no means a given, and the credit belongs primarily to one man; history will undoubtedly remember Dr. Dwight F. Damon as the Founding Father of Hypnotism as a profession.

Under his leadership NGH was the first organization to: develop a core-curriculum taught world-wide in a dozen different languages by certified instructors; establish an active legislative program to protect and advance the profession; establish universal standards of practice; formulate a professional language for hypnotists; establish a continuing-education requirement for certification renewals; provide definitive professional inclusions for publications such as Grolier's *Book of Knowledge* series and the Reader's Digest *Family Guide to Natural Medicine*. NGH is also the first and only hypnotism organization to receive recognition in the Congressional Record of the United States of America.

Continuing-education is provided for members and interested individuals at an annual convention and educational conference held each summer in New England; a smaller educational conference held each winter in Las Vegas: and, weekend seminars and workshops presented around the world on a regular basis.

Many Consulting Hypnotists are also members of the National Federation of Hypnotists, Local 104, OPEIU, AFL/CIO, CLC, a proud affiliate of the National

Guild of Hypnotists. Group programs and individual services are often provided for union members who are interested in smoking cessation, weight management and stress reduction.

There are a number of specialties practiced by consulting hypnotists, and many practitioners have gone on with their studies to also become certified in complementary medical hypnotism, clinical hypnotism, and to become NGH Board Certified. The practice of hypnotism is an emerging profession that encourages its practitioners to continue to seek and advance their knowledge.

NGH members deal with, vocational, avocational and self-improvement issues of individuals, areas of self-improvement that do not qualify as medical disorders or are not serious enough to be considered psycho-pathologies. In other words, consulting hypnotists work with ordinary, everyday people for ordinary, everyday problems. Medical, psychological and dental referrals are accepted as a complementary referral service to other licensed health professionals and their patients.

National Guild of Hypnotists members are held to a high standard of practice and code of ethics by our organization and we invite readers to contact us for referrals wherever they may be. Currently we have over 10,000 members located in 65 countries—possibly some right in your city. If you want an interesting speaker for your organization, someone to provide personal hypnotism services, or have any unanswered questions we are at: http://www.ngh.net.

Here are some simple explanations to help you as you read this publication: *Hypnotism* is the science, discipline or practice—*Hypnosis* is the phenomenon, or state of mind.

Hypnosis is a state of mind—it is the process of focusing an individual's attention while effectively communicating ideas that increase motivation and change perception—helping individuals to help themselves with issues related to normal problems of living.

Welcome to the wonderful world of hypnotism—

Donald J. Mottin, CMI, DNGH, OB
Vice President
National Guild of Hypnotists, Inc.

—World Headquarters—
National Guild of Hypnotists, Inc.
PO Box 308 Merrimack, NH 03054-0308
Phone (603) 429-9438 Fax (603) 424-8066
E-mail: ngh@ngh.net Web site: ngh.net

Chapter 2
What Is Hypnosis?

This is a difficult question to answer. Hypnosis has always been an enigma and is one of the wonders of modern psychology. No one really knows what hypnosis is. But then no one knows what electricity is either. Yet that is no hindrance to its usefulness.

In its most simple application, hypnosis can be a way of changing the mind. The classic dictum, "You are what you think," is so true. If we change the way we think we change ourselves. Mind is a process of producing thoughts, and when one is hypnotized it is possible to change the quality of thoughts—productive and helpful thoughts rather than unproductive and harmful ones. Hypnosis provides a means of directly reaching and influencing the subconscious mind. It is an amazing power.

To plunge a bit deeper and get more technical, it can be said that the mind tends to operate, more or less, on two levels, conscious and subconscious. The conscious level of mind is selective and critical of the thoughts produced, while the subconscious level of mind is non-selective and non-critical, hence is receptive to the subtle power of suggestion.

In relation to hypnosis, suggestion has been defined as being the subconscious realization of thoughts or ideas, often at such an ingrained level in the mind as to be beyond reaching through normal, everyday conscious control. Since hypnotic suggestion provides direct access to the subconscious mind, it is a means to achieve this desired control.

What is interesting is that suggestion is both the means of inducing the hypnotic state as well as controlling the state—often a point of confusion among even expert hypnotists as to where suggestion leaves off and hypnosis begins.

Reduced to its barest essentials, hypnosis can be regarded as a natural method of utilizing the innate receptivity of the subconscious mind to suggestion. The hypnotized person is hyper-suggestible. (Hypersuggestibility is an increased capacity to respond to suggestions.) It is thus that the hypnotist uses this state to redirect the mind of the client in the direction of desired thoughtful benefit.

Accordingly, it becomes obvious that the subconscious mind can be directed in a way that is beneficial to the hypnotized person, such as giving up smoking or other addictions. The suggestions given by the hypnotist will continue to be followed even after the client's return from hypnosis to the normal state of waking consciousness. In such posthypnotic operation of the continuance of suggestions lies the very essence of the value of hypnosis.

Weight control or weight loss, fitness exercises, good study and work habits, can all be motivated through hypnotic suggestion. Hypnosis is also effective in the control of pain, in the treatment of burn victims, migraine headaches, high blood pressure, chemotherapy side effects, warts, and psoriasis. Indeed, although hypnosis is not to be considered a cure-all, there are few medical conditions that cannot benefit considerably by hypnosis; and with none of the side effects of more common or traditional therapy.

Simple anesthesia, as for dental work and minor surgery, is not difficult to induce in the hypnotized person. It has been estimated that about eight out of ten persons can be readily hypnotized. As a rule individuals with an active imagination and of high intelligence can most readily enter the state. For use in major surgery it is generally felt that a deep level of hypnosis is desirable for the subconscious mind to block off intense pain sensations.

Through suggestion directed to the immune system, augmented by mental visualization, hypnosis has proved very helpful in fighting off invading viruses and bacteria as an aid in overcoming infections. For this purpose hypnosis is applied as an adjunct to conventional medical treatment, not as a replacement for it.

Hypnosis under proper guidance has excellent clinical value in psychotherapy. Many case histories indicate that not only can the psyche or spiritual part of a person be helped, through hypnotically induced suggestion, but also physical changes in the body can be influenced to occur.

Self-hypnosis is an important aspect of hypnotism to be considered. Since we can suggest actions ourselves to our own mind, it follows that it is possible to hypnotize one's self. Self-hypnosis brings the incredible force of your subconscious mind under your control.

John C. Hughes, DC, BCH, is Research Editor of the Journal of Hypnotism™. *He is the author of* The Worlds' Greatest Hypnotists, Hypnosis: The Induction of Conviction, and the Illustrated History of Hypnotism.

Chapter 3
How to Find a Referral

Are you looking for a referral? Where do you start? What questions should you ask? There are many good hypnotists throughout the country. But how do you pick one?

Let's start at the beginning. The best referrals come from someone who has gone to a hypnotist. You can ask them all types of questions and actually find out if the hypnotist helped them. If you do not know of anyone who has gone to a hypnotist, the next best thing is to seek out a reputable hypnotism member organization.

The National Guild of Hypnotists, Inc. was founded in 1951 in Boston, Massachusetts. We are the largest and oldest hypnotist member organization in the United States. Our member database holds over 7000 active members in the United States and 45 countries. We are continually striving to inform the public how hypnosis can help individuals who want self-improvement, such as smoking cessation and weight loss, and we also work with people who are nervous about exam-taking, flying and heights. People today are becoming more health conscious than ever before. Check out what hypnosis can do for you.

Call any professional hypnotism organization today and ask this one important question: How does one become a certified member in your organization? Every organization should have protocols, ethics and standards as high as ours. Call us and we can assist you in finding a referral in your area. Give our office staff the names of cities and towns within your traveling area and tell them the reason for seeking a hypnotist. For example, to stop smoking, for weight loss, relaxation or eliminating anxiety. Your giving us this type of information enables us to give you the best referral to a hypnotist in your area who may specialize in your needs. Ask for several referrals, so you can compare the information that you receive from each of the hypnotists.

The next step is to call these hypnotists. Make sure you ask some of the following questions: How long have you been in practice? What type of hypnotism training did you receive? Do you have any outside degrees (counselor, social worker, nurse, etc). Do you specialize in any particular area of hypnotism? (hypnobirthing, forensics, sports, etc.) What are your fees? How many sessions do you require for a particular problem? How long are the sessions?

There may be someone that you call that you do not feel entirely comfortable seeing without additional information. Ask what organization(s) they belong to. Call that organization and check on the status of that person. Not everyone belongs to a hypnotism organization. The more information you receive about the hypnotist, the more comfortable you can be when you make your choice.

Melody Bachand, BCH, was named Executive Director of the National Guild of Hypnotists after 20+ years of service in the world's oldest and largest professional hypnotists' organization.

You can call the National Guild of Hypnotists, Inc. at (603) 429-9438, or Email ngh@ngh.net or visit the Website, www.ngh.net, to receive referrals in your area.

Chapter 4
What to Expect on Your First Visit to Your Consulting Hypnotist

Expect to be greeted by a competent, confident, sincere and caring professional, who, by the way, is usually an excellent listener.

You will be asked to fill out appropriate paperwork about yourself to establish a base record of information in their office. After this you will be informed of what is universally called, the "Client Bill of Rights," which basically explains what services you can expect to receive as a client of that office. Most hypnotists will then tell you a bit about themselves, their qualifications, and what their approach is to helping you achieve with hypnosis.

Your hypnotist will also ask questions to draw out more information from you in order to custom design your session for your greatest personal success. For example: "Why, at this particular time in your life did you decide to make an appointment for hypnosis?" Or, "How will your life be different when you succeed and accomplish your goal?"

If you are seeing the hypnotist for a problem such as not being able to drive on the highway, you would probably be asked if there ever was a time that you could drive on the highway, to help your hypnotist establish a timeline to work with.

Your hypnotist is trained to draw out information from you to create a successful session as well as creating powerful, positive changes. So remember—if the goal is vague the effort is vague.

After completing their Intake Form consulting hypnotists will then carefully explain what hypnosis is in easy-to-understand terms. Perhaps asking if you have ever missed an exit while you were driving somewhere. Most of us have experienced this and can relate to it. It simply means that your mind was on something else, yet you were awake and in full control of your vehicle—just as you will be in hypnosis— awake and in control.

Do you recall day dreaming, staring at a campfire or the ocean, absorbed in a great book or listening to wonderful music, and suddenly it is several hours later and you thought perhaps only an hour had passed? This too is hypnosis. In fact, most of us are in and out of various levels of hypnosis on a daily basis.

Routinely, consulting hypnotists will ask, "Have you ever been hypnotized? — have you ever seen anyone else being hypnotized? Then they will discuss your impressions.

They will also explain such things as the fact that even though hypnosis parallels going to sleep you are not asleep when hypnotized. You can move in your chair, cough, sneeze, scratch an itch, yawn, and even speak if you have to, and nothing will disturb your hypnosis.

Your job as a client is to allow this wonderful experience to take place, not to make it happen.

Clients in their first session might have the thought that they are just sitting there with their eyes closed and nothing is happening. Your hypnotist will normally reassure you that you will automatically go to the level of hypnosis that you need for your individual success.

Your hypnotist will also tell you that you will hear all the outside sounds, but nothing will bother you or disturb you as they are just normal everyday sounds. Also, it is very normal for your mind to wander, so place those thoughts to one side and you can go back to them after your session is over.

You are in full control at all times and AT any time you could get up from the chair and walk out, but you would choose not to because it is such a relaxing experience.

After explaining items such as these and others, you will be given the opportunity to ask any questions.

Next, your hypnotist will do a couple of suggestibility exercises with you. These are also called conditioning or sometimes concentration exercises by various practitioners. They are not pass or fail type of tests, but simply tools to help the hypnotist to guide you to your success in your session . . . and they're also easy fun to do.

Now you are ready to experience hypnosis for yourself. The hypnotist reassures you that he or she will be guiding you through the session and giving the proper positive suggestions to assist you in making the powerful personal changes that you agreed to prior to your session. The hypnotist's work is always of a positive nature.

After your session you may be taught to do self-hypnosis. When the hypnotic session is completed you will be brought to full awareness by the hypnotist and as you emerge from hypnosis you will be refreshed, relaxed and feeling wonderful in every way.

Patricia E. MacIsaac, LPN, FNGH, CMI, OB, is the owner of the South Shore Hypnosis Center in Hingham, MA, and is a frequent lecturer and facilitator of workshops and seminars. She is certified to teach all NGH training courses, and is the recipient of the NGH Meritorious Service Award in 1993, Certified Instructor of the Year in 1995, Hypnotism Hallmark Award in 2006, and the Dr. Rexford L. North Award in 2007. She was also featured twice on the cover of the Journal of Hypnotism, *and is a member of the NGH Board of Examiners and Advisory Board.*

Patricia has taught, and applied the art and science of hypnotism to groups and individuals nationally and internationally. She can be reached at: (781) 749-9050, Pat@sshc.net, or visit her website: www.sshc.net

Chapter 5
Myths & Misconceptions

I'd like to clear up a few of the myths and misconceptions that the general public has about hypnosis. Most of the information people have received about hypnotism comes from TV, movies, and novels, and it is based more on old wives' tales or pure fantasy. Once in a while, in this age of tabloid magazines and the Internet, there are occasional stories of crimes being committed because the evil-doer hypnotized the victim. However, these fanciful stories usually take place in some far-off country where it would be difficult to check on the truth of the event ever happening.

Some Basic Facts About Hypnosis

Hypnosis refers to a state or condition in which the client becomes highly responsive to suggestions. There is hetero-hypnosis when a person is hypnotized by someone else, and self-hypnosis when a person creates the state on their own. However, the average person slips in and out of the hypnoidal state a dozen times a day. For example, daydreaming is a form of hypnosis; being "lost in thought" is a form of hypnosis; meditation, yoga exercises, and reverie, are all forms of hypnosis. The person is not asleep, yet is not awake, but is "in between" awake (beta) and asleep (delta); the "in between" being (alpha-theta according to what their brainwaves would show in a laboratory.

You Are Not Unconscious When Hypnotized

A major misconception is that the client is unconscious, but this is not true. Most clients can remember 99% to 100% of the hypnotic session after emerging. Hypnosis clients experience a pleasant, heightened awareness of sensations and usually relaxed and refreshed afterwards, They can converse with the hypnotist and remain hypnotized with their eyes open and could walk and freely move if asked to. So, you see, when people are hypnotized they definitely not unconscious or out of control.

You Will Not Become Stuck in Hypnosis

Another misconception is the fear of being "stuck" in hypnosis and not being able to wake up or come out of it. This is false because clients actually induce the trance themselves and can emerge themselves whenever they want to. In all reality, all hypnosis is self-hypnosis which is entered with the assistance of an experienced hypnotist to guide you.

You Will Not Reveal Your Innermost Secrets

Some people believe that while under hypnosis they can be forced to reveal secrets about themselves and others. This belief is not true because the client is aware of everything while being hypnotized. They can talk if necessary and could lie just as easily in the hypnotic state as not.

You Will Not Lose Control When Hypnotized

Because of how hypnotism has been portrayed, many members of the general public believe that hypnosis is somehow a surrender of the will and that they will submit to the "power" of the hypnotist. A hypnotist has no such power, and, as we said before, all hypnosis is self-hypnosis so clients actually hypnotize themselves and are capable of making decisions at all times.

Everybody Can Be Hypnotized

Actually, 90% or more of the population can be hypnotized to some degree and in some manner by an expert consulting hypnotist. In the matter of intelligence it has been found that people of average or above average intelligence are the best subjects. Persons who are unable to comprehend the instructions of the hypnotist because of being mentally incapacitated, speaking another language, being too young, or completely deaf would not be the best candidates, yet there are methods known to experienced consulting hypnotists which could possibly be used in any of these circumstances if needed.

Edward Morris, M.Ed.,CI, OB, has a degree in education and a resume that includes teacher, private school headmaster, guidance counselor, education director, and superintendent for the Maine State department of Mental Health. Ed has received the Instructor of the Year award, serves on the NGH advisory board and in 2006 was inducted as member of the prestigious Order of braid. Ed is a long time member of NFH Local 104, AFL/CIO, CLC, an NGH Certified Instructor and the Director of training for the NGH Institute headquartered in New Hampshire.

Chapter 6
What to Expect to Share on Your First Meeting With Your Consulting Hypnotist

The following intake information is vital for both client and hypnotist. As in all situations the information shared will be kept confidential and in a locked file cabinet between sessions.
In general the following information will be gone over between the two parties.

1- General vital information:
Give name, address, phone, email, employer, current work, education, other training, special aptitudes, date of birth, married, spouse name, responsible party for payment of fees, license number, general health, name and address of physician, etc.

2- Specific information:
Please note any medication or other preparations (e.g. multivitamins, herbs) and daily dosage.
What specific problem/situation brings you in? Please summarize briefly in your own words.
How did hear about us?
Have you ever been in counseling or psychotherapy?
If so, how long and with what results?
What would you say is your main concern at this time?
What would you be willing to let go of, or give up, to handle this concern, problem or situation?
What would you not be willing to give up to handle this concern, problem or situation?
Have you ever been in hypnosis? If yes, under what conditions and the results.
Have you ever seen anyone hypnotized? If so, how did you feel about that?
What was the response of others around you to the hypnosis?

3- To set the stage for the hypnotic session:
Please describe two of your favorite scenes or places, which symbolize to you good feelings such as peace, harmony, tranquility, contentment or relaxation. To aid clarity please focus on sight, sound, smells, textures, movement, taste, feelings on your skin (wind, clothing, etc.) and/or any other sensations or emotions each scene evokes.

4- Current Family:
To help us make the most of the time available to you, please complete each of the items below. If an item does not apply write in N/A. Your honest responses

will help us provide more efficient and effective service to you.
If presently married, spouse name and year married; name of prior spouse(s) & number of years married; names and ages of their children.

5- Medical History:
Note any conditions requiring hospitalization or outpatient treatment you have had over the past three years. Include dates and outcomes, conditions currently in treatment for and Doctor's name, location and phone #.

6- Family History:
Your family history may also be of value. Please respond to any of the following that apply to blood relatives & give the relation to you: problem drinking or alcoholism, substance abuse or drug addiction, bouts of rage, suicide or frequent attempts, depression or other emotional problems, difficulties requiring institutionalization.

7- Client Daily Life:
If you smoke or use tobacco, how much do you consume on an easy day & how much on a difficult day?
If you use alcohol, what form & how much do you consume on an easy day, how much on a difficult day? If you use mind altering drugs (valium, pot, diet pills, etc.) How much do you consume on an easy day & how much on a difficult day & name the drug(s), how many easy days do you have per week & how many difficult days per week?

In addition to these questions the client may have additional comments or concerns to discuss at this time.

Finally, before the sessions begin, it is important to establish an agreement such as the following:

8- Client Consulting Agreement:
In requesting professional consultation and assistance, I understand that to be successful I must be entirely willing to:
• Recognize that my health and well-being depend directly on how well I care for myself emotionally, physically, spiritually and intellectually.
• Acknowledge that my feelings, thoughts, images and desires, conscious and subconscious, ultimately determine the course of every action and relationship in my life.
• Realize that blaming anything or anyone, including myself, is totally useless and that the only person who can take charge of my life is I.
• Accept responsibility for myself, my choices and actions, and that I, knowingly or unknowingly, create them. Note: Responsibility means the ability to respond.
• Agree to be on time for my appointments, meet my financial obligations

promptly (including any session missed without a 48-hour notice), and participate wholeheartedly in the work I am undertaking.

I know my heartfelt commitment is an important first step in my work here, and my signature below underscores that commitment. If, in all good conscience, however, I cannot align myself fully with each statement above, I have initialed each acceptable item rather than signing at this time and agree to discuss in detail any reservations I may have.

Please Sign Client/Co-therapist
Signature: ______________________________Date: ________________

Consultant Consulting Agreement

In order to support you in deriving maximum benefits from our scheduled time together, I agree to:

• Use the best of my abilities and expertise to facilitate such changes as are mutually agreed to be in your best interest and in no way harmful to you.
• Work diligently to ensure as best I can that all suggestions given are positive in direction, beneficial in nature, and present within a context of health and well-being.
• Refrain from using you or your trust to satisfy any personal needs I may have outside of our working relationship.
• Offer you my undivided attention and professional assistance during our scheduled consultations.
• Inform you immediately if, in my judgment, you would be better served by another professional or an alternative/complimentary means of reaching your goals.

I am professionally committed to assisting you, in the shortest possible time and at the lowest possible cost, in mobilizing your resources to achieve maximum results.

Consultant/Therapist Signature: _________ Date: ___________

The above intake was developed by Anne H. Spencer, PhD founder of the International Medical and Dental hypnosis Association® for use with her clients and given to the students who graduated from her state licensed hypnosis training school in Royal Oak, MI. www.infinityinst.com aspencer@infinityinst.com

Chapter 7
Hypnosis for Rapid Results

It's a miracle! It works so quickly! I can't believe it's that simple!

These are some of the comments we receive on a day-to-day basis from students at the school and clients in the clinic.

We train many psychotherapists and doctors, who are always amazed at the speed of change when using hypnosis, particularly around fears, phobias, habit change or the feeling of "being stuck" in life.

The subconscious mind remembers everything that ever happened to you, from the get-go. It remembers what you learned at a very early age, either by direct teaching, or by osmosis. If you were born into a family which automatically assumes that women are lesser beings, or that you are always in the way, and are clumsy, and never do anything right, it becomes your truth, your version of the world. And we don't even know we're in that truth. A bit like a goldfish in a bowl, who doesn't know it's in water until you take it out.

That's how we are with early programming or training. We don't know our "water". We may think we do, (we always like to find the reason for something), but we don't.

Which is why hypnosis is so brilliant. It allows a professional hypnotist to facilitate your passage into an altered state, called a trance, so that the critical conscious mind can be set aside, or circumnavigated, giving access to the fabulous, powerful library and storehouse of your subconscious mind. Another magical part of the subconscious mind is that it doesn't know the difference between real or imagined. Try that out on someone scared of spiders or mice ... just mention you thought you saw one in the corner of the room, and notice their physical reaction as well as the verbal one! The body reacts as if it were real. Athletes use this phenomenon all the time, training through visualization.

And hypnotists use it for change.

And then what?

Ahh, that's what separates out the hobbyists from the professionals. In truth anyone can lead someone into hypnosis. It's what you do when they're there that makes the difference. The tools and techniques to make change or solve the problem are endless, and which one is used depends completely on the needs of the client. How do we know your needs? ... well, it's called an intake. The intake is the process which allows us not only to hear your story and what it is you want changed in your life, but also how you tell your story. Do you receive information in a visual way, or do you feel or have a knowing? Do you move towards something, or away from it? For instance, do you want to stop eating junk food, or start eating healthy life-giving foods?

All of this will tell your hypnotist the best tools and techniques to help you achieve your goal. Quickly and permanently.

All this input and how it is interpreted by your facilitator is essential for lasting change. Which is why it's imperative to find a hypnotist who has been trained by a credible, international organization like the National Guild of Hypnotists, Inc.

The general overall concept, once the client is in hypnosis, is to get to the root of the problem, by going back to the start of it, changing that original perception or decision, adding in a new decision and proposition for the future (which we call 'the script') and then taking you out to your future so that you can see and feel yourself as successful. Do that a few times, and behaviors change to match the new script, sometimes in as little as two or three sessions.

In the case of fears or phobias, these can be cleared in one session. There are many ways of doing this in hypnosis, but one of the most successful is the 10 step process by which you imagine yourself gradually moving up a scenario of least scary to most scary. With a trained, experienced facilitator guiding you through, there is no reason why you should be irrationally afraid of flying, spiders, public speaking, heights or anything at all. Just go to see your friendly hypnotist and let that fear go, quickly, easily and forever!

Dr. Georgina Cannon is a member of the NGH Advisory Board, a certified clinic hypnotist, an international award-winning teacher, and lecturer and director of a hypnosis clinic and school in Toronto, Canada. In the seven years since its founding, Dr. Cannon has initiated the ethical protocols and procedures for regression now followed by her students and many others in the regression field worldwide. Dr. Cannon also meets regularly with medical and wellness professionals to enhance their knowledge and awareness of hypnosis and the dynamic healing potential it offers.

Chapter 8
The Union and Hypnotism

The National Federation of Hypnotists, Local 104, Office and Professional Employees International Union (OPEIU), AFL-CIO, CLC, is the union that represents physicians, nurses, chiropractors, acupuncturists, podiatrists, midwives and other health care workers. OPEIU has represented hypnotists since 1980 and Local 104 has been in existence since 1994. Being affiliated with the CIO gives hypnotists a voice in political legislation at every level of state and federal government.

The union gives hypnotists a voice in government, and represents them before lawmakers. The union stands for fair treatment of all hypnotists. Hypnotists' credibility is important; union membership enhances that credibility by investing in the right to practice hypnotism.

Through hypnotists' membership they are making an investment in the profession they have chosen as life-long careers, and the union can provide the services that protect the legal rights members have earned and deserve. The union stands apart as a viable and relevant force in labor movements and will continue lobbying for issues that affect the hypnotists' profession on a state to state basis.

The union represents hypnotists by dedicating itself to gaining access to benefits to which they as hypnotists would not normally be entitled, such as union privilege benefits programs, i.e., legal advice and legislative affairs (ensuring Congress is aware of the members' positions on issues that concern their lives).

The National Federation of Hypnotists, Local 104 represents "solidarity." Because a hypnotist's credibility is important, the union enhances that credibility.

Sharon Morris, BCH, a Certified Hypnotist is a member with the National Guild of Hypnotists. She is also treasurer/secretary of the National Federation of Hypnotists, Local 104 - OPEIU-AFL CIO. She can be contacted at: hypnounion-sec@aol.com

Chapter 9
Hypnotism As A Career
National Guild of Hypnotists Training Programs

As Educational Director of National Guild Hypnotists, I've discussed hypnosis career opportunities with several thousand people from all walks of life and varied backgrounds–salespeople, unhappy with their jobs; teachers, tired of the school bureaucracy; housewives, attorneys, accountants, etc.–all looking, all searching for a new career that will be interesting, exciting and rewarding.

The profession of hypnosis represents a wonderful opportunity for individuals to be both conceptual and practical. It has been said in the field of education that people were practical but not conceptual or vice versa. Hypnosis allows people to be conceptual (creative – to have a big idea – the new thought) and to put it into practice.

Sound interesting? If so, here are some questions you should have answers for:

1. What training programs are offered and what are the requirements for certification?
2. Is there an opportunity to earn a good income as a professional hypnotist?
3. What about my personal growth?- What can I expect?

First, NGH requires a minimum of two college semesters (100 hrs) of training in basic and advanced hypnosis. NGH certified instructors offer core-curricula in basic and advanced hypnosis training which prepares participants to work privately or in groups with clients to help with problems such as smoking cessation, weight and stress management, career situations, sports enhancement, relationship problems and a host of other presenting problems. NGH certified trainers have had to participate in a rigorous training schedule that has prepared them to present the core-curricula in an interesting and professional manner. NGH has more than 450 certified instructors throughout the U.S., Europe, Canada, Asia and South America.

Richard Harte, PhD, FNGH, is a nationally recognized certified hypnotist and cognitive-behavioral therapist. He runs the Harte Center in New York. He has received the NGH Educator of the Year Award for 1991 and 1994.

Chapter 10
Self-Hypnosis

Self-hypnosis is the ability to influence our mind by our own positive (or negative) thinking. Self-healing can be accomplished through our voluntary acceptance and predetermined application of self-hypnosis.

Imagine—a personal computer, programmed to achieve a state of relaxation, eliminate stress, remove destructive habits or addictions, and improve athletic abilities. Or, wouldn't it be nice if we could push a button, transferring our negative thinking into positive and productive ideas, improving our physical prowess, accelerating our healing processes and preventing illness?

The reality—we already possess that almost magical computer—in fact, we are born with it. To be more precise, that computer is your sub-conscious mind and learning how to communicate with it can become an exciting and rewarding challenge. Using self-hypnosis, we can establish a communication circuit between our conscious and our sub-conscious mind.

Learned and experienced hypnotists have written multitudes of books on the subject of self-hypnosis. Others have been written by authors who write beautifully, but without the slightest concept of self-hypnosis, hypnotism or hypnosis.

A common question asked by prospective students interested in the study of self-hypnosis is, "I've read many books on the subject and I have followed their instructions, but it just doesn't seem to work for me. What am I doing wrong?"

Power and positive results of that imaginary computer, entrenched within each of us, can be expected if we are willing to practice the principals of self-hypnosis.

Possibilities, applications, and expectancies that are obtainable by the proper utilization of self-hypnosis are seemingly limitless. Think about it!

In the teaching of self-hypnosis, many hypnotists will advocate that an aspirant first experience a state of hypnosis by being tranced by a qualified hypnotist. The individual will then recognize the "feeling" associated with the trance state and develop a reference point in conjunction with his feelings while in a hypnotic state.

Hypnosis and self-hypnosis are a result of self-expectancy. It is essential that one should understand, specifically, what they could expect to both feel and experience when tranced as in the state of self-hypnosis.

Whenever engaging in a state of self-hypnosis, one is:

1. In complete control of one's state of mind.
2. Aware of what the tape recording is saying.
3. Always conscious.
4. In a state of concentrated attention.
5. Able to terminate the trance state at will.

Self-hypnosis will tend to cause positive improvements to become more permanent.Your mind accepts behavioral changes automatically, particularly because of the pleasure derived from the "better way." One would not wish to return to the outdated typewriter of yesteryear after being exposed to a sophisticated word processor. We prefer working in the easiest, simplest, and most improved manner possible.

All hypnotism is basically self-hypnosis. Nearly anyone can hypnotize himself or herself when they know how it is accomplished. We attain self-hypnosis by becoming influenced by our own thinking and that very factor proves our self-suggestibility.

In 1922 C. Harry Brooks wrote, "Every idea which enters the mind, if it is accepted by the unconscious, is transformed by it into a reality and forms henceforth a permanent element in our life."

To sum up, the whole process of self-hypnosis consists of two steps: (1) the acceptation of an idea. (2) Its transformation into a reality. Both these operations are performed by the unconscious. Whether the idea is originated in the mind of the subject or is presented from without by the agency of another person is a matter of indifference.

Through the benefits of self-hypnosis, we can learn to relax the body and mind, thereby causing ourselves to react more readily to positive suggestions. All sensible goals that we seek are realistically achieved through this media.

Medical information has indicated that 76% to 84% of our illnesses can be created by the mind and are referred to as psychosomatic illnesses. We must therefore remember that self-hypnosis becomes effective particularly when it receives its achievements from the programming of the mind. In short, what your mind has caused, your mind can cure.

Some of the names that self-hypnosis has been called are:

1. Self-hypnosis
2. Auto-suggestion
3. Auto-conditioning
4. Self-suggestion
5. Autohypnosis
6. Huna
7. Couism
8. Statuvolence

To paraphrase - If it walks, quacks, and looks like a duck... then it is a duck. So if - It sounds like, works like, and achieves the results of self-hypnosis then it is ... self- hypnosis.

Norbert Bakas, PhD, FNGH, has been practicing and teaching hypnosis and self-hypnosis for over 60 years. He is a BCH and a FNGH and an avid researcher and teacher of hypnosis and self-hypnosis both to his clients and the general public. He has taught over 100 courses in self-hypnosis in local colleges. He strongly advocates that all clients, students and hypnotists strive to be efficient in self-hypnosis.

Chapter 11
Weight Control and Hypnosis

Hypnosis and Weight Control

"You are becoming healthier, thinner and happier each day!" As you read and learn about hypnosis, it becomes very apparent that hypnosis is safe, natural and effective for behavior modification in many areas from athletic and academic improvement, smoking cessation and building confidence to more serious matters of physical and emotional healing. Hypnosis is also highly effective in the area of weight control. The vast majority of all people are by now well aware that changing behavior patterns to eat healthier and to engage in physical activity has been, is now and will always be the formula for weight loss and a healthier life. And still ... you just can't do it!

Why Hypnosis?

Every one of us can relate to that feeling of wanting to do something (exercise and eat healthy) but somehow we feel internally restricted. For some reason or reasons, the subconscious mind, which directs behavior, created and continues the act of using food for emotional comfort. Hypnosis is the highly effective process that expediently assists change for positive behavior for it is how to access the subconscious mind. As it has been written, "Ask and you will receive"... "... the answers are within." As the subconscious mind receives suggestions to eat healthier, be active physically and to feel more positive emotionally, those internal restrictions and barriers are reduced and eliminated, allowing the individual to have positive behavior changes that are life altering, achieving a healthier mind and body.

Behavior Changes Equal Results

The way hypnosis is effective is not directly related to weight loss, meaning, after a hypnosis session fat doesn't mysteriously disappear. The suggestions delivered to the subconscious during hypnosis direct behaviors to change, which in turn lead to the result of fat reduction/weight loss. Imagine feeling like you simply just don't want those unhealthy foods while at the same time having the desire to eat small amounts of healthy food. And when is the last time you actually wanted to exercise, to do things and be active? As the hypnosis is successful and these changes develop, the processes of the body that eliminate fat are now in high gear and that healthier, happier you will be in the mirror looking back proudly and gratefully.

Thomas Nicoli, PhD, CH, is a national television and radio guest and trainer in the field of hypnosis and hypnosis for weight loss. Email him at info@prosperusa.com and visit his web site www.prosperusa.com for more info.

Chapter 12
Medical and Dental Referrals for Hypnosis

There are times that a patient/client may want to address a medical or dental problem with the use of hypnosis. Indeed hypnosis has demonstrated effectiveness not just with psychological problems but for the treatment of many physical conditions such as digestive disorders, numerous cardiovascular, musculoskeletal and immunological problems. It has applications in pain management, surgery, dentistry and helping one undergo uncomfortable diagnostic or therapeutic procedures. Many modern hypnotists are well-trained in the area of medical hypnosis and hypnodontics.

Many medical professionals are aware of the current literature and recent studies showing the effectiveness of hypnosis; yet few mainstream doctors and allied personnel have sufficient training in hypnosis, let alone the time to implement this useful modality. A hypnotist will often be able to supply studies and articles to acquaint your doctor with the latest information as well as specifics on the procedure and its safety.

How might I get a referral? Your hypnotist may have a list of doctors (MD, DO, DC, PhD) who are willing prescribe hypnosis after a consultation. If you have already selected a hypnotist, she/he may want to contact the doctor for you and send follow up reports if indicated. Your hypnotist can often provide you with updated sources and studies to present to a doctor during your next consultation.

How can I get a referral from my doctor? How do I approach my doctor? For the benefit of the patient's well-being, many doctors are quite open to modern care that is safe, holistic and complementary to their work.

Your doctor may have a list of hypnosis providers the clinic already uses. Sometimes they may already have a certified hypnotist on staff or one who can come in to the clinic to perform such services. If your doctor or clinic already has someone on staff who does hypnosis on premises, it would provide concurrent care for you in a one-stop shopping environment. If it is an outside hypnotist of your choosing, you might want to have your hypnotist send follow-up reports on your progress.

What about health insurance coverage for these services?
This depends greatly upon the nature of the condition you are to have treated, your specific insurance policy and the laws of the region in which you live.

Dr. Bill Breuer, DC, CH, CI, FAPHP is the director of one of the oldest holistic complementary care medical centers, and has practiced hypnosis for approximately 40 years. He is the author of a medical textbook, Physically Focused hypnosis - A Guide to the Use of Hypnosis in a General Medical Practice *and a member of the National Association of Science Writers. Dr. Breuer has trained numerous doctors, nurses and mental health professionals and teaches a university course in hypnosis.*
Email: KyHypno@juno.com
Website: http://www.angelfire.com/ky2/multicare

Dr. Breuer is also the creator of the Hypnosis Museum, a medical center display of historical equipment and paraphernalia that can be visited online: http://www.angelfire.com/pr/hypno

Chapter 13
Hypnosis and Dentistry

Hypnosis is a wonderful adjunct to the practice of dentistry. It allows the dentist to teach the patient to relax during all procedures. This is important because of the sensitive nerves in the oral cavity, which can make even simple procedures seem uncomfortable.

Perhaps one of the best applications of hypnosis in dentistry is in the reduction of fears about the dental visit. If the patient is worried, tense and fearful the sensations felt during the visit are magnified in the patient's mind and are more bothersome than normal. When the patient is in a relaxed, calm and confident state of mind procedures are placed in a true perspective, not exaggerated.

Furthermore, the dentist may suggest changes in the patient's sensations by introducing suggested anesthesia. Not everyone can produce the suggested anesthesia to the same extent, but many can produce enough in the mouth to make the entire visit more comfortable. I have seen a patient who could make a molar tooth completely numb with self-hypnosis to have the infected tooth removed without other anesthesia, and without post-operative bleeding. The patient had been trained in self-hypnosis at an earlier date.

Other patients find they produce less profound anesthesia, but are not bothered by injections, dental drilling, and so on. The dentist may give the hypnotized patient a suggestion when the visit is completed that when he sits in the dental chair next time, he will feel a sense of relaxation and will, when the dentist says a "cue word," go into a deep state of hypnosis, deeper than today

At subsequent visits the patient will quickly go into trance, ready for treatment. This will save time for the dentist and the patient. These instructions are called posthypnotic suggestions, and may last for long times, for the patient's later benefit.

Patients of all ages can benefit from the use of hypnosis and dentistry. Children are often asked if they would be interested in a "game" which will make their visit more fun. They are usually excellent hypnotic subjects, and gain many benefits. Suggestion can help them stop bad habits such as thumb sucking, and nail biting. Improved brushing habits can be taught as part of their "game."

Hypnosis can help adult patients manage a new denture, or focus on prevention of new problems as needed.

Dentists trained in dental hypnosis find it facilitates their practice, and makes the treatments more pleasant for both Doctor and patient!

Jack Flanagan, DMD, Acton, MA, is now retired from the active practice of dentistry. He has devoted many years to researching hypnotism and dentistry and is a long-time member of the National Guild of Hypnotists. He has been a popular adjunct faculty member.

Chapter 14
Religion & Hypnotism

Religion and hypnotism have walked together from the earliest days of human history. Long before medical doctors or secular psychologists existed, shamans, temple priests, mystics and healers of all traditions understood and used the power of trance and suggestion. Contemporary hypnotists trace our history directly back to the 18th-century Roman Catholic priest, Father Gassner, whose work influenced Mesmer. While a few groups today still misunderstand the nature of hypnotism and therefore regard it with suspicion, most religious communities gladly use hypnotic techniques for prayer, healing, spiritual development, and personal growth.

Many religious professionals who use hypnotism are members of the Clergy Special Interest Group of the National Guild of Hypnotists, "an interfaith and educational organizations of professionals in God's service who prayerfully and responsibly use hypnotism as part of their ministry of compassion and spiritual healing." These men and women—clergy serving churches, synagogues, temples and mosques, or members of religious orders, or chaplains in hospitals, prisons, the military, pastoral counseling practices and other settings—believe that the loving God of all faiths wants every soul to move into ever-closer harmony with the Divine goodness, holiness and health. But we also know that such movement is not as easy as a simple act of conscious will-power.

Human beings like to think that they are in full, conscious control of their lives, but most of us know better. Our daily selves constantly get in the way of our better selves. We know we should take better care of our bodies, our minds, our spirits. Yet knowing we ought to do things differently is not the same as doing things differently!

As Saint Paul wrote, "I do not understand my own actions. For I do not do what I want, but I do the very thing I hate ... I can will what is right, but I cannot do it. For I do not do the good I want; but the evil I do not want, that is what I do." [Romans 7:15,19]

What Paul is describing is the human experience of psychological and spiritual entrapment in our own egos, our own unhealthful desires and urges, our delusions of conscious self-mastery, when in fact it is our unconscious mind that controls most of what we think we are choosing to do. The prayerful use of hypnotism allows us to get past our ego-selves and communicate effectively with our unconscious about what we truly need and want to do, to live in harmony with our highest, best selves.

What should you expect from a clergyperson who uses hypnotism in his or her work? Clergy who use hypnotism do so in the belief that this is a skill we are meant to develop and use. The particular techniques will vary greatly, but in general the religious use of hypnotism will involve metaphors and images from the practitioner's own faith tradition. Often prayer will be included, for guidance, protection and blessing. The goal is to change the beliefs of the unconscious mind in order to live in a more spiritually healthy way, to discern the will of God revealed within one's own soul, to make the best possible use of the gifts one has been given, and to change one's patterns of thought and action in order to live in harmony with the will and the love of God.

All of this is part of the life of faith. The partnership of religion and hypnotism is about changing lives for the better, in accordance with God's will.

Lindsay Bates, D.Min., CH, Senior Minister at the Unitarian Universalist Society of Geneva, Illinois, is currently President of the Clergy Special Interest Group within the NGH.

Chapter 15
Scientific Evidence and Hypnosis

Many people hold contradictory views of hypnosis. Some are fearful that the hypnotist can gain control over their will and force them to do things they do not want to do. Others believe hypnosis has no effect whatsoever on someone's behavior.

These beliefs are influenced by the number of ways we learn something is true.

We are influenced by what authority figures in our lives—parents and teachers and so forth—tell us is true. We are also affected by what makes logical sense to us. In addition, experience influences our beliefs. If someone has had a positive experience with hypnosis, for example, it helped them stop smoking, they believe it works.

The best way we know to demonstrate the true effect hypnosis has on people is to do scientific research. There are many ways scientists can do this research. They can do basic science research to study the core aspects of the hypnosis process.

They can do applied research by surveying people who have been hypnotized to measure the degree of effect of hypnosis. They can also compare the life changes of people who have been hypnotized with those who have not been hypnotized. The strongest measurement of the effectiveness of hypnosis occurs in studies where hypnosis is compared with another intervention for a problem.

Hypnosis has fared well in these scientific studies.

In August of 2000, scientists reported basic science research on the effect of hypnosis on the brain. Using a PET scan (Positron Emission Tomography), scientists saw changes in the brain activities of hypnotized subjects that did not occur in the non-hypnotized group.

The medical community has a history of using research to test interventions. Many doctors have long been interested in the use of hypnosis for medical problems and recently conducted many studies. In April of 2002, three doctors from England published the findings of their research on the use of hypnosis for irritable bowel syndrome (IBS).

They studied 250 patients who received 12 sessions of hypnosis.

All showed statistically significant improvement in gastrointestinal symptoms, quality of life, anxiety and depression.

The use of hypnosis to treat pain and anxiety are two areas of particular interest to the medical community. In both areas, hypnosis has been shown to be effective. In 2002, several doctors from Mt Sinai School of Medicine in New York City studied 20 women who were having excisional breast biopsy. The women who received hypnosis as part of their treatment had less pain and distress at a statistically significant level. On a 1 to 100 scale, with 100 being the most intense pain, the hypnosis group had a pain score of 15.48, the control group, 42.5. The distress score of the hypnosis group was 5.97, the control group, 28.0.

Another group of doctors from Beth Israel Deaconess Medical Center/Harvard Medical School studied 241 patients having invasive vascular and kidney procedures. The 241 patients were divided into three groups: one group of 79 patients received standard care, another structured attention and the third group of 82 patients was given hypnosis. The subjects in the hypnosis group had better pain control, less anxiety and fewer complications than either of the other two groups.

Scientific research also continues to be done on the effectiveness of hypnosis to treat a number of common challenges like smoking and weight loss. This research will continue to give feedback to hypnotists as to the most effective ways to work with clients for these issues.

Madelaine Lawrence, PhD, Certified Hypnosis Instructor, is the published author of a book, many articles and a hypnosis newsletter on scientific studies of hypnosis. Email her at lawrencecenter@sbcglobal.net.
website: www.lawrencecenter.net.

Chapter 16
Hypnosis vs. Psychotherapy

Many people are unaware of the differences between hypnosis and psychotherapy.

They may even integrate them in their minds into one area known as therapy. There are major differences that consumers should be aware of when contemplating therapy. The following thoughts are offered in the hope of a better understanding for consumers concerning these differences.

hypnotist: one who was trained in the principles and methods used to develop trance and to use the phenomenon of trance as an intrinsic part of the hypnotic process in affecting growth and change for the client in a positive way.

The process involves:

1. The development and expression of thought and imagery.
2. The ability to stimulate memory recall.
3. Enhancing the client's capacity to quickly develop and emotionalize reports with the hypnotist/hypnotist.
4. A tremendously heightened ability to internalize the new and different ideas presented by the practitioner utilizing a variety of hypnotic methods.
5. Heightened potential for stimulation of memories and attitudes.
6. Accessibility to levels of deductive processing.

Hypnosis

Hypnosis training begins with the teaching of trance development, followed by the utilization of the "phenomena of trance" and a wide variety of hypnotic techniques for rapid movement toward the client actualizing goals.

Hypnosis is a naturalistic approach to the use of the client's present resources and strengths to further the accomplishment of meaningful goals.

Hypnosis is usually presented as a dramatically rapid intervention system which strengthens and reshapes the client's feelings of competence and capability (one or two sessions is not uncommon). The hypnotist works in the area of the mind that is best for finding the causal factor to ascertain why the client has not attained the goals he/she has been striving to reach.

In most states hypnotism is a non-licensed profession. The consumer should not misunderstand this statement. Non-licensed does not mean non-legal. It simply means there is no licensing by the state for the profession. There are hypnotism laws that must be adhered to in most states by any practitioner of hypnotism.

Hypnotists are usually certified members of a national hypnotism organization.

This membership indicates they have successfully completed the necessary educational requirements to meet the standards of a particular organization. The largest and most prestigious of these organizations is the National Guild of Hypnotists.

Among non-licensed practitioners of hypnotism there is no label attached to clients.

The practitioner works on the issue the client has brought forth in the pre-induction interview. There is more privacy and confidentiality because in most cases insurance companies are not an issue.

Psychotherapy

Training in psychotherapy begins with and is strongly influenced by Freudian psychoanalytic theories.

Traditional psychotherapy holds the view that virtually everyone has some form of neurosis which emerges as part of a developmental struggle to socialize a primitive, aggressive and often destructive pool of energy referred to in psychotherapy as the "id." In other words, as one psychotherapist once put it, "If you're not in therapy you're in denial."

Psychotherapy strongly implies that therapeutic change is usually difficult and time consuming and therefore requires extended therapy, 10-20 sessions. (Two or more years of regular therapy sessions are not unusual.) In most states psychotherapy is a licensed profession. It is usually licensed under a state board on mental health which may also have specific requirements for a psychotherapist utilizing hypnotism as an adjunct to psychotherapy. Since it is an adjunct to the profession, it is not generally utilized on a full time basis as it is with the full time hypnotist.

Psychotherapists are trained to work within the confines of the conscious mind. It is generally understood that the conscious mind basically has four functions: the analytical function, will power, temporary memory and rational function. The attempt to correct behavior using these constructs at best is extremely long term.

The hypnotist knows the goal is to bypass this area and work within the area of the mind (subconscious) most appropriate for locating the cause of an issue. For all practical purposes, the hypnotist/hypnotist functions as an organic computer reprogrammer. By understanding this concept it is easy then to understand the real differences between hypnosis and psychotherapy.

Gerald Kein, CI, FNGH - Omni Hypnosis, Deland, FL is acclaimed by many as one of the leading instructors of clinical hypnotism. He is a Board Certified Hypnotist with the NGH.

Chapter 17
Differences in Titles – Certified Hypnotist, Consulting Hypnotist, HypnoCounselor

A rose by any other name ... an appropriate description for the absence of a difference among these three titles. Many words, phrases and titles evolve over a period of years in all professions, some through widespread usage, and others through design of the professionals that adopt them. The word "hypnosis" was coined way back in 1850 by a medical doctor by the name of James Braid. It is a Greek derivative which means "sleep," but is really a misnomer as hypnosis is not sleep, and Braid would have liked to take back this nomenclature. Nevertheless, from hypnosis came the practice of hypnotism; thence the practitioner being called a hypnotist.

After the invention of chloroform in 1854, hypnosis took a back seat and was not really medically or clinically revived until acceptance by the medical profession in 1950.

During that inactive period the name hypnotist was usually applied to entertainers who used hypnotism on the stage. In the early 1980s, teaching institutions began offering hypnosis certification courses and awarded graduates with the title of Certified Hypnotist. When acceptance of the clinical use of hypnotism by the public began to snowball, the title of hypnotist was thought to be more applicable to the services offered, as the benefits of hypnosis became readily apparent not only with smoking cessation and weight management, but as highly complementary to the medical field.

Then, in 1993, along came disputes between practitioners of hypnotism and psychologists in several states. In New Jersey, there was an agreement reached with the New Jersey Board of Psychological Examiners resulting in a formal exemption being granted for the practice of hypnotism provided that the title hypnotist was no longer used in New Jersey. This writer is the author of that exemption and suggested that the title "hypnocounselor" or "certified hypnotist", "hypnotist", or "consulting hypnotist" replace the title of "hypnotist," at least in New Jersey.

The end result is that when you see a title of certified hypnotist, hypnotist, hypnocounselor, or consulting hypnotist that is utilized in relation to the clinical practice of hypnotism, they all have the same meaning.

Tony De Marco, LLB, is co-founder of the Academy of Professional Hypnosis, approved as a post-secondary vocational school by the Department of Education of the State of New Jersey, and is the author of an addictions practice manual for professionals entitled HypnoAddictionolgy—Slaying the Dragon of Addiction. *He may be contacted via email at nickeby@aol.com*

Chapter 18
An Easier, Safer, More Comfortable Birth—

Imagine That!

At a time when we are witnessing a push from within the medical establishment for earlier induction of labor, increased use of epidurals, and an alarming incidence of Cesarean sections, a relatively new birthing program that is fast gaining the attention of birthing professionals and the media all over the world has come to the forefront.

This new kid on the childbirth education block uses the registered trade name HypnoBirthing®, a name that a few decades ago would have evoked skepticism, if not outright ridicule, from pregnancy consumers and medical care providers alike.

This is not the case today, however. The name notwithstanding, pregnant women from all over the world are being drawn to this program in droves. As many as two thousand women find their way to the HypnoBirthing® website each week. Between four and five hundred contact the HypnoBirthing Institute®, located in Chichester, New Hampshire, to seek a referral to a practitioner and sign up for the five-session childbirth education class. They are not looking for a magic hypnotic trance that will take them away to some distant place during labor. They are looking to HypnoBirthing® to show them and convince them that birthing is normal, natural and healthy, and that they can birth their babies into the world safely, without drugs and with a minimum of discomfort.

They quickly learn that HypnoBirthing® is as much a philosophy of birth as it is a birthing technique. It is a total shift in paradigm from what is considered the norm in birthing today. Most approaches to using hypnosis in birthing are based on the premise that the pain of birthing can be masked. With HypnoBirthing®, women are taught the true physiology of birth. Mothers learn that their bodies are created to give birth, just as their babies' bodies are created to assist in birthing. Once a woman understands that there is no pathological reason for pain in childbirth they are ready to learn to use self-hypnosis to bring themselves into that profound state of relaxation that allows their bodies to function in the way that nature intended.

The key to HypnoBirthing® is actually "de-hypnotizing" to help parents rid themselves of the myths that surround birthing. Certified HypnoBirthing® practitioners are facilitators, teaching women to relax, to release their fears, and to use the remarkable power of their own minds to imagine and create the image of positive, gentle birthing. The process is so simple it is almost unbelievable, and the results are causing people in medicine to take notice.

The main goal is to help parents raise their awareness that birth does not need to follow the medical model, and then teach them through guided imagery and a carefully thought out program of special breathing that to give birth in a safe, easy, and comfortable manner is within the realm of their imagination.

Marie Mongan, MEd, RH; of NH and AZ is an award winning therapist with over 30 years of experience. She is a licensed counselor, is certified as a hypnotist and hypnoanesiologist and is nationally recognized instructor of Hypnobirthing®.

Chapter 19
Medical Hypnotism

Most people are surprised to learn that the American Medical Association approved hypnotism as a valid tool in health care in 1958. In actuality, the recognition was overdue as the hypnotic arts and sciences had long been an accepted part of health care practices in Europe.

Because hypnotism was brought to American in the 19th century by traveling Mesmerists who made outlandish claims, and because those claims were picked up in popular fiction by well-known novelists, the public perception of hypnotism in America had become flavored with the atmosphere of the side-show. However, beginning in the 1930s serious scientists began to investigate the value of hypnotism, and by the 1950s the case was made. Hypnotism can help in your health care efforts.

First, there is abundant evidence that hypnotism can help in the management of pain. While most people think of pain as something in the body, actually pain is in the mind. Pain is an interpretation made by the brain of impulses arriving from the nerves. Hypnotic suggestion can affect how that interpretation is made. Just as one person might find the taste of a hot pepper upsetting while another finds it delicious, a skilled hypnotist can use suggestion to alter the interpretation your mind makes of a painful stimulus so that it is less of a problem. Similarly, suggestion can be used to "magnify" the beneficial effects of pain medication so that good results can be achieved using a lower dose, causing less side-effects or sedation. Even truly chronic pain conditions such as fibromyalgia, dental problems, arthritis or chronic fatigue can be helped.

Second, hypnotism excels at helping people with any medical condition that has a stress-related or psychosomatic component. Irritable bowel syndrome, headache disorders, dermatological conditions, cardiovascular disease and autoimmune disorders such as lupus are only a few of the conditions that benefit from the kind of deep relaxation a properly hypnotized person feels.

Finally, a hypnotist can help you maintain a healthy lifestyle that can prevent medical problems from arising in the first place. Your hypnotist can assist you in smoking cessation, weight management and motivation for exercise. He or she can even assist you in remembering to take needed medication on time, and if you need surgery your hypnotist can sooth away pre-surgical worry so that your time in the hospital goes well.

When seeking a hypnotist for assistance for a health-related issue, care should be taken to seek a practitioner who offers complementary medical hypnotism (from the root-word for "complete") instead of some form of alternative medicine. A properly trained hypnotist will provide hypnotism only as an adjunct to the care you are receiving from your doctor. It will not be used as an alternative or substitute for that care. The goal of any properly-trained hypnotist is to help make the care you receive from your physician more effective. The goal is never to replace the work of your physician.

As very few medical professionals are adequately trained in hypnotism, if you decide to explore what hypnotism can do for you, help can be sought from a practitioner certified by the National Guild of Hypnotists. Guild hypnotists are held to high standards by their certifying organization and will provide only complementary care. When a person consults a hypnotist for assistance with a health-related issue, the practitioner will need a referral from a physician or other licensed health-care professional. As more and more physicians are aware of the value of hypnotism, your doctor will almost certainly issue the referral on your request.

The Rev. C. Scot Giles is a Doctor of Ministry, a Board Certified Chaplain and a Fellow of the National Guild of Hypnotists. He directs the first hospital-based, medically approved program in America for the hypnotic treatment of cancer and is the author of the National Guild of Hypnotists curriculum in Complementary Medical Hypnotism. His web site is http://www.counselingministries.org and can be reached at CSGiles@uuma.org.

Chapter 20
The Art Of Forensic Hypnosis

A forensic hypnotist is viewed within our profession as a specialist, and rightfully so. When the Council of Professional Hypnotist Organizations (COPHO) first addressed the various disciplines of hypnotic applications, forensic hypnosis was given significant recognition.

They compared this specialty within the field of hypnosis to brain surgery within the field of medicine. A forensic hypnotist is an expert level craftsman. The art and science of this discipline mandates advanced training and a specific mindset apart from other procedures.

Forensic hypnosis has been well defined by Hibbard & Worring as the application and management of the science of hypnosis in criminal and civil investigations.[1] The primary objective of forensic hypnosis is to enhance the memory and recall of volunteer victims and witnesses to crimes and civil actions. However, recent U.S. Supreme Court decisions have extended this application to include assisting defendants and defense witnesses.[2] Published authorities of memory and hypnosis agree that all sensory input taken in by our five senses is recorded somewhere in the brain.

They also recognize that much of this information is originally perceived and registered only on a subconscious level. Some information may register consciously but often just slips away from conscious awareness because we probably labeled it as too unimportant at that time to be of value. Some traumatic memories may even be suppressed because they are just that, too traumatic. Human safeguards come into play when that happens. The good news is that experts also believe that these stored memories and information can largely and accurately be retrieved through the use of hypnosis, even in those instances where they were perceived as too traumatic or too unimportant.

A Few Cases in Point

One of the more famous examples of the effectiveness of forensic hypnosis occurred in 1976 in Chowchilla, California (*Time*, September 13, 1976, p. 56). It is to date the largest mass kidnapping case in history, anywhere in the world. Three young men, wearing ski masks and brandishing weapons, kidnapped a school bus with 26 children and the driver. The bus was stopped on a makeshift detoured rural road and all of the victims were herded into two vans. They were driven to a stone quarry a hundred miles away and, one by one, placed inside an abandoned semi truck trailer that had been buried six feet underground. The town of Chowchilla tripled in population overnight with reporters and federal investigators. The town ran out of food and water. A hotline was connected to the White House where the president was given constant updates. Some 16 hours later, the captives were able to dig themselves out and were rescued. Questioned by the FBI, none of the victims could provide identifying information about the suspects.

A hypnosis session was conducted by Dr. William S. Kroger with bus driver Frank Edward Ray. With this assist, Mr. Ray was able to recall all but one digit of the license plate on a white van used by the kidnappers. This information led to the arrest of the three kidnappers. To date the Chowchilla kidnapping has been made into two movies, one of which stared veteran actor Jack Klugman as bus driver Ed Ray. This event has also been the subject of countless TV special reports.

In another case, a brazen rapist in Texas would go from door to door from 3:00 am until 9:30 am.[3] When an open door was found he would enter, rape and assault his victim. One victim, however, was stabbed multiple times and left for dead. After the assault she could not remember anything about her assailant. However, under hypnosis, she was able to assist an artist in the construction of a composite drawing of the assailant and recalled everything he had said during the commission of this crime.

When the suspect was apprehended, the information that had been obtained under hypnosis was compared with other facts and everything obtained under hypnosis was essentially corroborated. As a point of information, the suspect later confessed to a number of murders and over 60 rapes.

Numerous examples of this valuable investigative tool have appeared in the media.
This author utilized forensic hypnosis to solve a brutal "cold case" murder that occurred 21 years ago. (*News-Dispatch*, "Solved ... after 21 years," April 13, 2003)

What Is The Difference Between Forensic Hypnosis and Clinical Hypnosis?

Forensic hypnosis and clinical hypnosis are two very separate and distinctive applications of hypnosis. Each of these has their own unique objectives significantly well apart from each other. Clinical hypnosis utilizes hypnosis exclusively for therapeutic applications. Its main objective is to use hypnosis to enhance the process of therapy with a client. This could be for an emotional, medical or psychological concern.

Forensic hypnosis sessions, on the other hand, must be conducted completely void of any therapeutic applications. Their prime focus is to utilize the science and art of hypnosis to aid the client's memory and recall of issues often critical to a criminal or civil investigation. The session must be conducted in an expert manner and to a degree that can withstand legal scrutiny by the courts and other experts.

There are other significant differences between the way clinical and forensic hypnosis sessions are conducted that are absolutely crucial. Clinical hypnotists enjoy the normal doctor-patient type of relationship. They have the comfort and security of working alone in a private office and few, if any, outside individuals will ever see their work product or even their client notes or records, for that matter. Forensic hypnotists, on the other hand, are required to have their sessions video recorded continuously from the moment they say hello to their client until they say goodbye and the client leaves the office. Good trance depth is required and appropriate tests have to be demonstrated to verify the depth level achieved. Then all the reports, tapes and related material must be preserved as evidence. Like all other scientific evidence, this session may be scrutinized by opposing experts. Eventually, the forensic hypnotist may be called upon to testify in court, experiencing all the activity associated with that.

Clinical sessions are normally conducted in multiple sessions, perhaps three to four one-hour sessions. The therapy may even extend well beyond four sessions and perhaps into months or years. The forensic hypnotist, however, is usually pressured into obtaining crucial information on a particular investigation in a single session that may extend anywhere from four to six hours. The information he or she can gain through the use of forensic hypnosis is often too critical to take days, weeks or months to obtain. Also, the forensic hypnotist is seldom called upon to work on a minor issue.

Their request is always to help obtain information on a capital offense or some other major concern.

Qualification Is The Key

Professional authorities agree that forensic hypnosis is not for amateurs or experimenters. It is an advanced serious specialty within our field and requires specialized training and certification in some states. It requires a broad knowledge of hypnosis sufficient to be qualified as an expert in hypnosis. The hypnotists' level of competence needs to be able to withstand the scrutiny of opposing experts and attorneys. Their practice skills must follow high ethical standards. All authorities, including the Council On Mental Health of the American Medical Association, agree that clinical hypnotists, regardless of their medical degrees, status or experience, should not attempt forensic hypnosis unless specifically trained in this discipline. [4]

SUMMARY

Forensic hypnosis has assisted in the successful investigation of numerous major cases throughout the country. It has helped obtain license plate numbers of getaway cars and provided descriptions of attackers, robbers and murderers. At the same time, it has saved lives and averted false imprisonment for others. It uncovers missing information and helps solve crimes. Forensic hypnosis presents to the public hypnotism's most serious professional face. Because of their advanced training, experience and credentials, the forensic hypnotist is recognized most everywhere in the legal and professional world as a highly skilled competent practitioner, and an expert in the field of hypnosis.

George H. Baranowski, FNGH, is considered a veteran in the field of hypnosis with over 25 years experience. He is regarded as one of the leading experts in the field of forensic hypnosis and has assisted in the successful investigations of numerous major crimes across the country. He holds the status of Fellow with the National Guild of Hypnotists. George has been a featured columnist in the Journal of Hypnotism™ *since 1989 and is an advanced instructor. mindsightconsultants@comcast.net.*

References

1. *Hibbard W., Worring R.,* Forensic Hypnosis, The Practical Application of Hypnosis in Criminal Investigations, *1981*
Thomas Publishing (P. 3).
2. *Scheflin A., Shapiro J.* Trance on Trial, *1989 The Guilford Press, (p. 111-114) Rock v. Arkansas*
3. *Reiser M.,* Handbook of Investigative Hypnosis, *1980 LEHI Publishing (p186).*
4. *Council on Mental Health: Medical use of hypnosis.* American Medical Association Journal, *168(2):187, 1958.*

Chapter 21
Pediatric Hypnosis

What Is Pediatric Hypnosis?

When most people hear the term pediatric hypnosis they assume that it is simply normal hypnosis applied to children. Nothing could be further from the truth. Rather than hypnotize a child using adult techniques, we use a magic crystal (a method to hypnotize them that they believe in) and take them to their magic mind (that part of their mind where they go often and make believe). We talk to children in terms they understand and the children call us the hyp-y-nosis doctors. This magic mind of a child technique is effective from about three years of age into the teen years, depending on the emotional level of the child. I'm certain you can think of a four-year-old child that acts like an adult and an eighteen-year-old that acts like a four-year-old.

Why Is Pediatric Hypnosis Used?

If, in your mind's eye, you could see and hear a three-year-old talking about the Tooth Fairy and then see and hear a thirty-year-old talking about the very same subject you would understand why adult hypnosis doesn't work with children. The adult expression is based on logic and the child's expression is based on feelings. For example, a four-year-old recently told me that her mother said the Tooth Fairy was beautiful but the little girl didn't think so. The little girl felt that the Tooth Fairy couldn't have a pretty smile because all the teeth she had would be different shapes and different sizes. (Think about that, adults.) By using the magic mind technique I contact a third party (the magic mind) that knows everything there is to know about the patient and will share the information with me. The magic mind will also tell me how to resolve the problem in a manner that fits the child's belief system and is therefore acceptable to the child. It's just like magic.

How Can It Be Helpful?

Because children live almost all of their lives through feelings and not logic, taking them to their magic mind allows me to tap into the child's feelings and make powerful changes. For example, if your child doesn't like school you might tell that child the law says they must attend school; or they must go to school now to go on to higher learning; or they must go to school now to make a good income when they are older. It simply has no effect on the child. This is logic; kids work with emotions. If we take that same child and, through the magic mind technique, create a good feeling about going to school, the problem is resolved. Just some of the issues that can be quickly resolved by using the magic mind technique are bed wetting, hair pulling, nail biting, all fears, ADHD, fear of the dark, grades, test taking, sports, relationships, and on and on.

Donald H. Rice, CH, with several offices in Phoenix, AZ., has been a certified hypnotist for over twenty years. He often appears on television and radio, where he promotes hypnotism. Mr. Rice has taught and certified over one thousand people including forty-one psychologists, twenty-four psychiatrists and hundreds of medical doctors. He would be happy to hear from you by email azdrice@cox.net.

Chapter 22
Hypnosis and Study Skills

Hypnosis can be used to enhance every aspect of studying and can assist a person to achieve their academic and vocational goals. There are many factors involved in the process of studying. Initially, the individual must understand the purpose of the process that involves seeing the subject to be studied in a wider context. For example, it is common for school children to struggle in subjects that they see as irrelevant, but as this is a perception issue, it can be altered by looking at the situation from different angles. The environment of learning is also important, both in terms of physical surroundings and emotional support. If these are inadequate, hypnosis can enable the person to make the best of their own situation, and recognize the control and choices that they do have. It is then more straightforward to choose behavior that is appropriate to meet the desired goals.

Hypnosis can also assist the individual to develop belief, not only in their ability to learn, but also in the possibilities that such learning opens up. Once they have this belief, they will have the confidence to study. We all have far more "brain power" than we will ever use. Once an awareness of capabilities has developed, choices become clearer, rather than allowing limiting beliefs to restrict the scope of possibilities.

If belief, purpose and environment are in place, it then becomes a natural process for motivation to develop, as the pleasures of success are more apparent. Also, the more a person enjoys the subject itself, the more they will be intrinsically motivated, and the more meaning and commitment they will give to the process.

It is often recognized that there are three key stages of learning. Each step can be aided by the use of hypnosis, as follows. The first stage involves gaining an understanding of the subject at a conscious, cognitive level. For example, if learning a foreign language, this stage may involve learning the translation of words and rules of grammar.

The second stage is the associative phase, wherein elements are put together. Using the foreign language example, this may involve being able to construct a sentence from the components of nouns and verbs, etc., learned in stage one. Hypnosis can assist in the processes involved in these steps by encouraging understanding and clarity.

The third stage is known as the autonomous stage, and it is at this point that the knowledge "sinks" into the unconscious and becomes automatic. For example, this is the stage at which a person can simply say something in a foreign language, without specifically having to translate. Hypnosis can speed up this process of unconscious integration and allow it to happen more smoothly.

Hypnosis can then be used to aid concentration, understanding, memory and recall, particularly by the use of hypnotic mental rehearsal. If anxiety is a factor, perhaps connected with taking exams or the prospect of failure, hypnosis can also help alleviate the symptoms and reframe possible outcomes, leading to a more relaxed and helpful mode in which to work.

Fiona Biddle, FNGH, has been in practice in England since 1993, and is currently Executive Director of the National Council for hypnosis (UK) and Principal of the UK Academy of Therapeutic Arts and Sciences. www.fionabiddle.co.uk

Chapter 23
Hypnosis in Geriatrics

One of the miracles of the 21st century is that almost three decades have been added to the life span of the average person in North America, and that is the equivalent of an entire generation. In 1900 the typical North American lived to the age of forty-seven. Today that number is seventy-six. Not only are people living longer, but they are also enjoying healthier, more vigorous lives than even most younger people experienced in 1900. The aging generation is no longer the rocking chair generation!

Yet many of those seniors are lonely, depressed and in pain, and others suffer the anxieties of insomnia, losing control of their lives, maintaining driving skills, rehabilitation after surgery, sexual inadequacy, and a host of other difficulties that accompany the aging or maturing process.

Hypnosis and self-hypnosis in expert hands can certainly help seniors to achieve a positive and optimistic outlook on life. Peace of mind and activity go hand-in-hand towards creating a senior's happy life, and those who enjoy fun and laughter and a positive self-image are generally the happiest.

The hypnotist can play a most important role in not only helping the geriatric patient to relax, have fun and enjoy life, but also to actually guide the golden ager to exercise daily (using his physician's guidelines), to get involved in the community, to share distress with a friend or family member, and to find joy in keeping up with friendships, relationships and current events.

One great advantage that hypnosis offers is bound up in the nature of hypnosis itself. Seniors readily understand the relaxing, stress reducing nature of hypnosis, particularly when a simple and easily comprehensible explanation is given by the therapist. Our clients' favorite is, "When someone relaxes a bit, and we can get their attention for a short while, they then happily become very receptive and responsive to suggestions that they approve of."

We also emphasize that they will always be wide awake and totally in control of themselves, and it is also pointed out that hypnosis is never a sleep.

The applications of hypnosis for the elderly are boundless. Where stress is a factor, techniques of hypnosis will teach the sufferer how to relax and then deal with the stress-creating situation. Where loneliness is present, the therapist using hypnosis helps the patient to socialize and feel confident with others. In retirement homes where loneliness and depression are prevalent, the hypnotist can organize group sessions in which specialized relaxation techniques are taught. Participants learn a total mind-body relaxation which they can then practice both in group and when alone. This leads to a self-hypnosis skill with participants learning to successfully make self-suggestions, and then take more control over their lives. The results are generally quite spectacular. Elderly participants begin to walk more and to enjoy some exercise. Sleeping and eating habits tend to improve as energies are being directed to more activities. Courses given by the police or fire departments on senior safety are attended with attention and enthusiasm, as knowledge creates power and confidence. Rehabilitation exercises, both mental and physical, are tackled with the spirit of getting better, and the pain control abilities of hypnosis can, in many cases, be applied.

A joy of living, a positive, involved and active lifestyle, plus a more healthful life can do so much to bring peace and harmony to the golden-agers' world. In the experienced and well trained hands of a specialist, hypnosis can offer many benefits to the geriatric patient and help change the rest of his/her days ahead.

Maurice Kershaw, MA, FNGH, Dollard Des Ormeaux, Quebec, Canada, is a hypnotist and college professor in Quebec, Canada and has been in hypnotism since 1952 when he founded his full service therapy centre. He has been a member of NGH since 1952, he is Chairman of the NGH Board Certification Committee and recipient of the Rexford L. North Trophy for 2001.

Chapter 24
Smoking Cessation

Today's consulting hypnotist is most likely to hold a valid certification of extensive training in hypnosis from a well recognized hypnotism organization like the National Guild of Hypnotists which has more than 10,000 members in 65 countries worldwide.

Hypnosis has become recognized as one of the most effective tools to help smokers who want to quit. Fortunately there are many effective techniques in the profession dealing with smoking cessation. The one that I prefer to use is to educate the client as to the effects and consequences of cigarette smoking, just before I start with the hypnosis induction.

Smoking causes approximately 440,000 premature deaths in the United States annually, leading to more than 13 years of life lost for male and female smokers. Cigarette smoking has been associated with all types of sudden cardiac death in both men and women, and smoking-caused coronary heart disease may contribute to congestive heart failure.

Also, smokers are at an increased risk of getting mouth and pharynx cancer. Also, lung cancer is second only to heart disease as the leading killer of smokers in the United States. However, giving up smoking even late in life eliminates most of the lung cancer risk and many of the other consequences of smoking.

Hypnosis involves inducing a state of comfortable relaxation, and then directing the individual's attention to a particular strategy that will empower him or her to stop smoking and live a longer and much healthier life.

The focused concentration and heightened suggestibility of the trance state helps the client accept the hypnotist's directions. It also enables the client to develop stronger willpower and self-control—tools essential to eliminate the smoking habit.

Research has shown that it is not necessary to go into a deep trance to reap the potential benefits of the hypnotic state. Often, in fact, the greatest gains are made by those in only a light or moderate trance.

Since smoking injures almost all bodily organs and tragically these injuries almost always lead to incurable disease and death, so it is of great importance that anyone who smokes stops this self-destructive habit, before it is too late.

Hypnosis is a modality of choice for many people and the results are very encouraging as more and more people overcome the smoking habit through the use of hypnosis.

Although hypnosis is not a "magic wand," thousands of people have found that it can produce impressive results in the proper hands—especially for smoking cessation—in one or two short sessions.

Over 150,000 Americans smokers are affected with lung cancer and more than 90 percent will die from it. Lung cancer frequently produces no early specific symptoms and often spreads to other organs in the body before being detected on x-ray. Tobacco tars have been repeatedly proved to cause lung cancer.

One of the more common conditions created by smoking is emphysema. Tobacco smoke coats the tiny air sacs in the lungs with tars, causing the delicate tissues to lose their normal elasticity, after years of being stressed and stretched these air sacs enlarge, breakdown, and become useless for breathing. The smoker must stop before becoming crippled.

Jacob Bimblich, BCH, FASH, OB, is an acknowledged pioneer in the field of hypnosis smoke cessation techniques. He was named NGH Member of the Year in 2003, received the President's Award in 2005, the Hypnotism Media Award in 2008, and is an inducted member of the prestigious, Order of Braid.

As an award-winning motivational speaker and hypnotist, Jacob Bimblich has been guest lecturer at numerous colleges, universities, and medical centers. He has been featured on numerous Spanish-language CDs and DVDs, and his bi-lingual articles and columns have been published in leading professional publications.

visit him at: www.jacobbimblich.com email: hypnomotivator@gmail.com

Chapter 25
Diabetes & Hypnosis

Diabetes is now classified as a worldwide epidemic. Blindness, kidney disease, impotence and many other illnesses are often the direct result of out-of-control or undiagnosed diabetes.

Fortunately there are several ways hypnosis can help. See which one of the following statements applies to you or someone you know. (1) As a person with diabetes, do you feel stressed? (2) Are you the parent of a child with diabetes? (3) Do you wish that you, your child or spouse were more motivated to exercise? (4) Wouldn't it be great if it were easier to make better food choices? (5) Is your diabetes causing embarrassing personal problems?

Now since a hypnotist is, by definition, a stress management consultant and a motivational coach, all of the above challenges can be powerfully addressed by using hypnosis, but please note the following: a hypnotist is only part of your diabetes support team. Always be sure to have your doctor's approval before beginning any hypnosis program that can have any influence on your medical condition.

The primary method by which hypnosis helps a person with diabetes is by reducing harmful stress. There are two fundamental ways in which stress negatively affects a person with diabetes: (1) Stress robs a person of necessary personal power that is crucial in giving a person the emotional ability to make choices that benefit their health and well being. (2) As a diabetic's stress levels increase, so does their blood sugar. This is due to the "fight-or-flight" response that people experience as a result of negative stress. When a person enters this state of mind, their body releases chemicals known as "insulin-antagonists." These chemicals temporarily block the action of insulin while simultaneously causing the release of stored sugar in the liver and muscles.

With the above understanding about the two ways that stress affects a person with diabetes, let's see how that information, specifically point one (as point two is self-explanatory) then applies to the five problems listed in the second paragraph.

Regarding statement one, it is obvious to anyone with diabetes that having that disease is very stressful. This harmful state of emotional affairs then makes it difficult for a diabetic to follow their doctor's recommendations. Also, when a person is in emotional pain, they usually reach for whatever makes them immediately feel better. This can be any addiction, though it is usually food and typically too much and not the kind that is good for a person with diabetes.

Looking at statement two, it can be noted that stress packs a powerful double punch for parents of children with diabetes. This is because first, the parent is stressed out caring for an ill child and second, the child has overwhelming stress because they are not as equipped as an adult to deal with the enormous responsibility of successfully managing their disease. The parent must also then have to deal with their child's stress. This double-whammy makes it very difficult to achieve the kind of precise care that is needed for good childhood diabetes management.

In statement three, the fundamental issue is exercise. Since 95% of all persons with diabetes have Type 2 and since 90% of all those persons are obese, the implications for enhanced exercise motivation are all too clear. For example, it is well documented that many Type 2 diabetics have had complete symptom remission after achieving a significant reduction in weight typically due to exercise and diet improvement. Additionally, exercise greatly contributes to one's sense of well being and this therefore becomes a positive motivational cycle.

Statement four addresses a concern that many people have, not just those with diabetes. "I wish I could just eat better!" is a familiar refrain. Again, as a hypnotist helps a person to reduce their feelings of stress, they can then help that person to strengthen their inner commitment to making better food choices. Please note that even a small reduction in a diabetic's long term blood sugar tremendously reduces their chances of having serious complications later on.

Statement five refers to conditions that are difficult for most people to talk about. For brevity's sake this discussion is limited to one very common embarrassing problem; impotence. Nearly 60% of all males with diabetes experience impotence. There are two concerns here: (1) There is a good chance that these people and their partners are feeling a great deal of unnecessary and harmful stress. (2) A male diabetic may choose to take a medication for impotence when that medication is inappropriate and quite possibly harmful. This concern is also relevant to those millions of men with undiagnosed diabetes.

In conclusion, an NGH trained hypnotist can be an important part of a diabetic's health care team by helping a person with diabetes effectively reduce their stress.

C. Devin Hastings, CH, is a Type 2 diabetic who had almost total vision loss due to diabetes twelve years ago. He now has 20/20 vision because he applied the healing benefits of hypnosis as described above. If you have any concerns or need more information, please visit him at www.mindbodyhypnosis.com or email him at: devin@mindbodyhypnosis.com

Chapter 26
Hypnotism and Sleep Problems

Statistics show that insomnia affects 60 million North Americans and very often it is the root cause of many physical, emotional, mental and spiritual health problems. There is, however, a simple and effective way to get a restful night's sleep—use hypnosis to put insomnia to sleep.

What Is Insomnia?

Insomnia is defined as a habitual lack of sleep. It is a disorder, with an external and internal cause. External causes may be due to physical exhaustion or the consumption of stimulants such as coffee, tea, soft drinks, or alcohol and /or drugs. If insomnia is largely due to external causes then you need to take the appropriate steps to correct them.

First examine your sleep patterns, and determine if the issue requires medical attention (chronic depression, sleep apnea, physical pain). You'll also need to examine your diet, exercise patterns, sleeping environment, personal habits, lifestyle and worries.

In most situations insomnia is caused by a subconscious emotional traumatic event(s) that took place in the past. Usually the client is unaware of these events at a conscious level. That is when hypnotic work with the subconscious can help.

What Hypnosis Can Do For Insomnia:

Hypnosis is a natural state of mind. It is the safest drug-free way to alleviate insomnia.

Hypnosis bypasses the negative self talk of the mind and can uncover the subconscious root cause of insomnia. This will lead to a more productive life.

Through hypnosis we can help the client to use the power of the subconscious mind in order to relax and promote sleep.

Why Is Hypnosis The Answer To Insomnia and How Does It Work?

First we need to understand how the mind works.

The mind can be separated into three parts: the conscious, subconscious and the unconscious.

The conscious part of the mind is analytical, rational thinking and holds short term memories. The internal chatter that occupies a person's mind and which blocks them from going to sleep is in the conscious mind.

Within the subconscious mind are our emotions, beliefs, feelings, habits, and worries. It also operates like the hard drive of a computer.

Then we have the unconscious mind, which operates the automatic functioning of our being which is affected by the conscious and the subconscious.

The most prominent causes of insomnia are negative emotions such as the fear of dying, fear of the future, anger toward unresolved situations or people, worry, sadness, guilt, grief, and stress.

Another major cause of insomnia are the limiting beliefs we have such as: "I am not feeling safe, I cannot sleep, no one loves me, I'm not good enough," etc.

Thus the main source of insomnia is found in our negative emotions, beliefs and feelings, which are all stored in the subconscious mind. If you ask an insomniac what is happening when he/she lies in bed, they say that their mind will not shut down. A thought pops into their head and then another, and before they know it their adrenaline rises and sleep becomes difficult. This creates more stress, causing less sleep, and the cycle continues.

Self-hypnosis is a powerful tool that can help a person to achieve peaceful sleep.

Self-hypnosis will enhance your sleep by mentally focusing your attention on each part of your body. Start from your feet and move all the way up to your head. One way to relax your body and calm your mind is to first focus on a specific part of your body and then relax that area by taking a deep breath and imagining that you are removing all the tension that is stored there. Continue until you have finished with each body part. Start from your toes, and work upward to your head. Any tension in your body will soon drain away.

Another way of self-hypnosis is to have the hypnotist anchor "triggers," such as rubbing two fingers together, that will activate a peaceful, deep sleep. After learning this through self-hypnosis, you can relax yourself by simply rubbing your two fingers together. This powerful technique can work for you anytime you want peaceful sleep.

Yes! You can put insomnia to sleep with hypnosis by accessing and reprogramming your subconscious emotions and beliefs.

Debbie Papadakis, BCH, CI, Sleep Deprivation hypnotist Expert, psychotherapist and the founder of the Hypno Healing Institute, Inc. She teaches a variety of courses in the field of hypnotism, including certified hypnosis courses sponsored by the NGH. She also runs a private hypnosis practice in Toronto, Canada. Contact her at the Hypno Healing Institute Inc. 355 Keele Street, Toronto, Ontario M6P 2K6 416.760.8996. 1.888.758.3223.
www.hypno-healing.com info@hypno-healing.com

Chapter 27
Significant Effects of Hypnosis on Creativity

Hypnosis has significant effects on creativity. This is the conclusion of a three year research project conducted in conjunction with the Department of Visual Arts, Department of Theatre and the Psychology Department at North Dakota State University.

For the past 3 years, Chair of the North Dakota State University Psychology Department Dr. Jim Council, Professor Pam Chabora of the Theatre Department, several psychology graduate students, art undergraduates and myself have researched the significance of hypnosis on creativity. We have studied painting and drawing in the visual arts as well as acting in the theatre arts. In all cases we have found the effects of hypnosis significantly influence creativity.

During my fifteen years of teaching, I have explored numerous teaching methods aimed at getting students to think outside the box and be more creative. My goal in applying these different methods involves opening students up to new ideas, guiding them to understand they are creative individuals with unique insights, sensitivities and ideas. Assisting them to discover their personal poetry, skills and confidence is my function as an art educator. I have found hypnosis to be an important, fun and significant tool in accomplishing this goal.

The effects of hypnosis include: 1. Assisting students to relax, 2. Relieving them of inhibitions and self-imposed limitations, 3. Relieving them of fears and 4. Aiding them in improving their self-esteem.

1. Hypnosis relaxes students, resulting in a state of high receptivity.
Usually in a studio class, concepts, ideas and the elements of art are presented through lecture/demonstration. Even though students pay attention, their minds wander. Relaxing them with hypnosis aids them in focusing on what is said.

2. We impose limitations and inhibitions upon ourselves. Suggestions to go beyond these limitations and release ourselves from inhibitions are made during the hypnosis session.

3. Artists, and most notably young artists, deal with a certain amount of fear—fear of putting themselves out there visually for others to see, fear of the materials, fear of looking stupid and, like they don't know what they're doing or they don't know what to do. Specific hypnotic suggestions assist in relieving these fears.

4. Hypnosis assists students with self-esteem. In the induction, students are asked to visualize touring a museum. Works described during the visualization include masterworks the class has shared.

Suggestions made include having fun with ideas and the medium like masters. You, too, have good ideas and make marks as they have made.You, too, are a master artist. These suggestions build confidence and simplify the art making process by reducing it to "making marks." We can all make marks and arrange them in our own way.

It is my conclusion, after hypnotizing hundreds of students, that we all have a wealth of creativity stored within us. Hypnosis doesn't give one the knowledge or ability to be an artist. It guides one to open doors to the depth of creativity within us. Hypnosis can assist in relieving ourselves of inhibitions, self-imposed limitations and fear, clearing the way to create with that ultimate freedom we seek as artists.

Kimble Bromley is an associate professor of art and coordinator of the Department of Visual Arts at North Dakota State University in Fargo, ND. He teaches painting and drawing. Bromley has exhibited his art work regionally, nationally and internationally. He has held painting residencies in Chicago, Cuba, Ecuador, Jamaica and Mexico. He received the North Dakota State University College of Arts, Humanities and Social Sciences Creativity/Research Award in 2003. Bromley received his hypnosis certification from the National Guild of Hypnotists in 1999. He can be reached at: (701) 231-7824, Kimble.Bromley@ndsu.nodak.edu
www.ndsu.nodak.edu/instruct/bromley/self-esteem

Chapter 28
Pain

"Ouch! Pain Costs Employers $80 Billion Annually"
Summarized from a Reuters Health/ABC News Story,
August 21, 2002

A 34-year-old woman presents with constant disabling headaches of two years after hospitalization with Louisiana Encephalitis. No more headaches after hypnosis.

A 24-year-old young lady was referred with a three-year history of Fibromyalgia. Six hypnosis sessions later she was back to running five miles a day and pain free.

A 31-year-old nurse referred with severe suffering from Tic Douloureux. She had over 99 severe hot poker shooting pains from her cheek to her eye daily. After three visits she went from 99 very painful tics a day to 1-2 non-painful twitches per day.

The list goes on. Constant post surgical bladder pain for two years is now pain free. Back pain for five years - now pain free. Neck pain three years - pain free. Cancer pain two months - pain free. Stating it simply, "Hypnosis works." It has a very high success rate while being non invasive and free of harmful side effects. "Side effect" may include sleeping better, feeling better, less stress, healthier eating, enhanced immune system and, best of all, the feeling of having control of one's pain.

Pain Defined

According to the American Pain Society (APS), pain is an "unpleasant sensory and emotional experience associated with actual or potential tissue damage, or described in terms of such damage." Pain is the number one reason that Americans seek medical attention. Approximately one out of three people are diagnosed with chronic (recurring) pain each year.

Why Hypnosis?

Whether using medication or hypnosis, the goals of controlling pain are to limit suffering, preserve hope, and restore participation in life activities. Only hypnosis, however, addresses both the sensory and emotional aspects of pain.

What the Experts Say

* Hypnosis was endorsed in 1958 by the American Medical Association (AMA) as an adjunct in a multidisciplinary setting or as stand-alone therapy for pain management

* National Institutes of Health (NIH) panel has stated evidence that hypnosis is

effective in alleviating chronic pain associated with various cancers, irritable bowel syndrome, inflammatory mouth conditions, temporomandibular disorders, and tension headaches

*Joint Commission Accreditation of Health Care Organizations (JCAHO) Standards place special emphasis on non-pharmacological methods of pain management, which includes hypnosis.

Techniques that can be used to reduce or eliminate pain are:

*Direct suggestion to lessen pain that may include creating glove anesthesia (numbing of the hand, which can be transferred to the painful area)
*Relaxation using progressive relaxation and direct suggestions
*Distraction by engaging the attention on something other than the pain. The focus is on a safe place, a hobby, a vacation – anything that is a distracting image and appeals to the person in pain.
*Displacement, which is transferring pain from one area of the body to another.
*Dissociation of pain, which is the ability to become detached from the immediate environment.

Summary

Hypnosis has a multi-centennial history as one of the first and foremost enduring modalities in pain management. Its effectiveness is documented based on the research of notable universities such as Harvard, Yale, Stanford and Columbia. In proper perspective, hypnosis may not only relieve pain, but also help to maintain the dignity and well being of the client or patient without dependence on large quantities of medications.

CAPT Ron Eslinger, US Navy Retired, Certified Registered Nurse Anesthetist, is a Board Certified hypnotist and Hypnotherapy Instructor through the National Guild of Hypnotists. He is published in multiple nursing journals and is a sought lecturer to nursing organizations. He is presently CEO Healthy Visions Wellness Center. 865-220-0777, www.hypnosisforpain.com.

Chapter 29
Hypnosis in Sports

Hypnosis has a long history in sports performance enhancement, especially self-hypnosis. (A reminder, all hypnosis is self-hypnosis.) In the 1943 *Journal of Applied Psychology*, Dorothy Yates of San Jose State College reported her use of mental "set," which she described as a "waking trance," with college boxers. Since then the popularity of hypnosis use in sports has endured a similar fate as hypnosis use in public perception—it has been described as everything from a medical miracle to outright quackery. Recently, hypnosis in sports is enjoying a more positive image. The Association for the Advancement of Applied Sport Psychology (AAASP, n.d.), which is the recognized body for the science of applied sport psychology, now lists hypnosis as one of the nine modalities it endorses for enhancing performance in athletes.

This recent sanction of hypnosis is more a measure of acceptance of the term than of the use of hypnosis as a mental skill modality. Since the 1970s sport psychologists have been teaching a variety of visualization exercises to athletes to enhance performance. Many of these visualization exercises, especially mental rehearsal, are performed in a relaxed state and quite often the athletes experience hypnotic trance states by accident or on purpose. In this state of self-hypnosis, the routines and behaviors are strongly imprinted upon the subconscious so that when it comes time to perform, athletes can more easily move into flow, recreate a flawless routine, or exhibit remarkable creativity in their performances.

Visualization is a staple of sports mental skills training packages (Reese, 2004). Vadcoz, Hall, and Moritz (1997) list five types of imagery (visualization) utilized to enhance performance: motivational general imagery for self-confidence, cognitive specific imagery for rehearsal of skills, kinesthetic imagery for movement awareness, arousal imagery for levels of cognitive anxiety, and mastery imagery that combines cognitive specific imagery with motivational general imagery to enable the practitioner to take control of the kinesthetic visualization. Regardless of the type of visualization, the addition of hypnosis can improve its effectiveness.

Teaching focus and concentration is another specialty area of mental skills training. What better way to encourage focus than with a modality that is, by definition, a focused state of attention? Beyond improving focus and concentration, hypnosis can assist athletes in accessing peak experiences and flow state—often referred to as the zone. Flow is an elusive mental state in which "one becomes totally absorbed in what one is doing ... So flow is about focus. ...

flow is a harmonious experience where mind and body are working together flawlessly." (Jackson & Csikszentmihalyi, 1999, p. 5) The main difference in the description of flow state and the hypnotic state is that hypnosis is not elusive and can be summoned on command.

Teaching athletes to access flow on command is the Holy Grail of applied sport psychology, and hypnosis can assist. In a recent scientific study (Pates, Cummings, & Maynard, 2002) on the effects of hypnosis on flow states and three-point shooting performance in basketball players, results showed that all participants increased both their average three-point shooting percentage and their average flow scores calculated on the Flow State Scale developed by Jackson and Marsh (1996). In addition, each athlete reported that the hypnosis intervention was valuable for maintaining confidence and staying relaxed and calm during competition.

When used by itself or as an adjunct to other mental skills like goal setting, visualization, energy management, effective thinking, and mental toughness, hypnosis can be an especially effective intervention technique that can have an immediate and positive impact on athletic performance. (Reese, 2004)

References:

AAASP. (n.d.). Applied sport psychology: Psychological skills definitions. Retrieved March 25, 2004, from http://www.aaasponline.org/asp/skills.php

Jackson, S. A., & Csikszentmihalyi, M. (1999). *Flow in sports: The keys to optimal experiences and performances*. Champaign, IL: Human Kinetics.

Jackson, S. A., & Marsh, H. W. (1996). Development and validation of a scale to measure optimal experience: The Flow State Scale. *Journal of Sport & Exercise Psychology*, 18, 17-35.

Pates, J., Cummings, A., & Maynard, I. (2002). The effects of hypnosis on flow states and three-point shooting performance in basketball players. *The Sport Psychologist*, 16, 34-47.

Reese, B. (2004). *Develop the winner's mentality: 5 essential mental skills for enduring success*. Philadelphia: Xlibris.

Vadocz, E. V., Hall, C. R., & Moritz, S. E. (1997). The relationship between competitive anxiety and imagery use. *Journal of Applied Sport Psychology*, 9(2), 241-253.

Bob Reese, MA, ATC, CH, served as an athletic trainer in the NFL for 25 years. He is an assistant professor of psychology at Jefferson College of Health Sciences in Roanoke, VA. Bob and his wife Joan facilitate enduring success through their peak performance consulting firm Reese Resolution Services. Contact Bob through the RRS website: www.reeseresolution.com

Chapter 30
HypnoCoaching™

Would you like to live a life that is rewarding, yet balanced? A life with a specific direction where you're achieving more and reaching or surpassing your goals, yet always staying aligned with values that are truly important to you?

HypnoCoaching™ can help.

The concept of personal coaching may be the hottest new direction for self–improvement in the new millennium. Just as sports coaches can help athletes win gold medals, personal coaching helps people achieve their personal goals. Twenty or thirty years ago, it may have been in fashion for people to be in therapy to deal with everyday challenges and issues. Now people want real results in their lives, and they realize that if they don't have clinical mental or emotional problems, weekly therapy may not be what they need.

Traditional therapy tends to focus on the past, and talking about the reasons for problems and issues. Coaching focuses on the present and moving toward the future to help one become more successful, be more productive, and lead a happier, fuller, more balanced life. Hypnosis has been around for hundreds of years as an effective way of tapping into the power of the mind to help people create lasting changes in their lives. More recent tools for change such as NeuroLinguistic Programming(NLP), made famous by people such as Tony Robbins, have been used successfully in conjunction with hypnosis for decades now. HypnoCoaching™ is an exciting new method which combines the best of personal coaching with the amazing powers of hypnosis and NLP.

HypnoCoaching™ begins by helping you to identify your core values, to determine what is truly important to you. Then you begin to set life goals that are aligned with your core values to help you create an amazing future. Together with your coach, you'll analyze your life balance, design action plans and strategies, and begin moving forward toward making your dreams become reality.

Your coach helps you stay on track and move forward, keeping your life in balance.

Together you'll work out ways that you can set priorities, get past obstacles, and stay motivated while achieving your desires, to help you be the best that you can be.

Your coach is an advocate for helping you achieve what's important to you, without having his or her own agenda—the kind of support that is often hard to obtain from family, friends and co-workers. Along the way, you'll be supported by having regular interactions with your coach. HypnoCoaching™ is very flexible—you might interact with your coach by phone, in person, or by email, or some combination. Your coach helps you fit coaching into your busy life, and will help you come up with a schedule and format that works for you.

As a regular part of your encouragement and support, your HypnoCoach™ will provide you with the extra advantage of using hypnosis. Hypnosis can help you internalize beneficial attitudes and behaviors which contribute to your success. Instead of having to "try" to do things, hypnosis can help positive habits and attitudes become automatic for you. Self-hypnosis can also be used to help with stress control, ability to focus, staying motivated and many other issues. Some people have certain obstacles that have held them back in the past, such as a fear of public speaking, or a lack or self-confidence, or getting past procrastination. Those kinds of issues can be difficult to get past with other kinds of coaching, or by someone trying to "talk you into it," or telling you to "get over it." These issues (and many others) are the types of behavior changes that hypnosis can help with, quickly, comfortably and easily. This is another specific benefit of HypnoCoaching™—it's like turbo-charging your results!

Lisa G. Halpin, DCH, BCH, is a Board Certified hypnotist, and the originator of HypnoCoaching™. She is also an Advanced Certified Instructor for the National Guild of Hypnotists, providing training to professional hypnotists. Her website is www.hypnosisdoctor.com.

Chapter 31
Parenting and Hypnotism

Has your child felt frustrated during life challenges? Have you wondered what you could say and do to help your child to endure (and to keep your sanity through the challenge)? If so, it all begins with hypnosis.

I remember one time being with my son when he was ten-years-old. We were waiting in the laboratory for him to have blood work done. He began to cry. He didn't want any more needles.

As a heart patient, he donated his blood for testing too often. He never liked being stuck, and we did the best we could do to support him through it.

This time, I did my best to reason with him. I said, "I wish we didn't have to do this either. I know you've already said you need to do this the squirmy way. So, go ahead and cry if you need to and you can hold my hand tight. Keep your arm straight while you're giving some blood to the lady. We'll just get this over with as fast as we can."

Almost any time we express strong emotion, we have hypnotized ourselves. We can effectively help our children cope with trauma ([feeling upset] and in a hypnotic state of mind) by speaking in encouraging ways. When we focus on what we can do or have during a perceived unpleasant situation, we focus and concentrate on possibilities instead of limitations. When we focus on what we can't do or can't have during an unpleasant situation, we create a feeling of hopelessness and stay mentally stuck in limitations. So, to cope with unpleasant or unwanted situations we accept what is happening and find ways to harmlessly work with the situation.

After the blood draw ended, we talked about Jason's feelings. I listened without belittling, shaming or humiliating him for his feelings. He said, "I didn't like that. I don't like needles."

I said, "Yes, I didn't like watching you go through it all. But I noticed how brave you were. Did you notice that you were brave?"

Jason said, "I noticed, but I didn't like doing it."

I said, "Yes we both agree on that point. I feel happy and proud you are my son. Do you feel proud of what you did?"

He said, "Proud? I'm just proud it's all over!"

Why do we want our children to achieve? Because we love them. When our children are hypnotized during trauma, we want to help them HARMLESSLY cope with an unpleasant situation.

Harmless coping means we offer them no food (or external substances) as a "reward" for being so brave. Adding food to the scenario only creates a thought pattern process that might lead to them becoming overweight.

Harmlessly coping means we add no punishment as a result of them expressing their true feelings about a situation. Children do have the right to feel upset sometimes. When we acknowledge that something is unpleasant and that they did achieve a goal, we show them we value and respect them as individuals.

Harmless coping means we encourage them to draw from internal strength to effectively cope and work with unpleasant situations. By encouraging them to do their best, we provide healthy models of responsibility for them. In this way, our children benefit by learning to find healthy ways to succeed during life.

Do you have a child you'd like to help succeed? If so, when they feel upset work with their natural and normal hypnotic state. Encourage them rather than minimize them so they can create and develop a healthy, productive method of coping with life traumas.

An internationally known, accomplished and highly respected hypnotist, trainer and writer, Susan Fox earned certification in hypnotherapy in 1988 at the Hypnotism Training Institute of Los Angeles, California. Susan specializes in self-empowerment programs. She uses hypnosis and her vast understanding of how to talk to the buying part of the mind in marketing programs and for people experiencing chronic pain. She lives with her husband, Rudy, and second born son, Keenan, in Ohio, USA.

Susan writes a column called "Hypnotherapy Scripting" for the Journal of Hypnotism™. *She received the 1998 International Hypnosis Hall of Fame's Woman of the Year Award. She was nominated to receive the 1998 Sealah Award and induction into the International Hypnosis Hall of Fame. She can be contacted by e-mail at hypnoresearcher@yahoo.com.*
Please see her website at www.sleepwhilesomeoneelsesnores.com.

Chapter 32
Taking Control of Your Fears

As a young wife and mother, I had many fears. They controlled my life. I couldn't eat in restaurants, go to parties, or even attend my children's soccer games without an intense feeling of despair. I would feel nauseous and faint, and would want to run away.

I tried to reason with these feelings but could not. They made no sense to me or to anyone else. Someone told me to try hypnosis. I wasn't sure about it, and even thought it might be scary. I couldn't have been further from the truth. After leaving the hypnotherapist's office, I thought, "Well that was relaxing but I was wide awake and aware of everything. How could this possibly work?"

It worked fantastically well! In fact, it forever changed my life. I never had those negative feelings again. My life opened up. I was able to go out, travel and yes, eat in restaurants! I soon realized that I wanted to become a hypnotist and help others.

Today as a practicing hypnotist, I now view fears very differently. It is amazing how we develop them and how simple it can be to get rid of them.

Uncontrollable fears can be developed in many ways. Perhaps they begin with a situation, person or place. It could be a movie, or even a book that we read. Perhaps they are brought on by attention or even developed as a way to protect us.

As children, we can develop fears simply by watching one of our parents react to an event that might be frightening to them. A father is walking with his daughter. He crosses the street to avoid a dog up ahead. Even though he is not verbally expressing a fear of dogs, his behavior does. The daughter picks up on the behavior and brings this into her adult life where she may even pass it on to her children.

They can also develop as a result of something fearful that was instilled in us by another person. I recently helped a man get over the fear of needles. Under hypnosis it was revealed that when he was younger, his mother used to keep him in line by threatening to take him to the doctors for a shot if he was bad. When I questioned him about how his mother felt about doctors he responded that she absolutely hated to go to them. To her it was a punishment.

I have even found in some instances that when a client realizes where the fear started, they can then quickly move away from it. This is especially true if the fearful initial event was actually not scary at all but just a misunderstanding. This can happen in children when they witness a situation between adults that they, as children, perceive differently.

So how do we overcome fear by using hypnosis? In essence, we take that negative feeling and emotion and change it into a positive one by "anchoring" it on a positive experience. The next time we are faced with the same situation, we now respond in a more positive manner. We feel better about the experience and feel more confident and self-assured.

Cynthia Kile Thomas is founder of the Thomas Institute of Hypnosis in Manchester, New Hampshire. In her office, she sees clients for private sessions and travels to corporate settings for group sessions. Cynthia also teaches students to become certified hypnotists at her institute. You can learn more by visiting www.thomashypnosis.com

Chapter 33
Entertainment & Hypnotism

This article concerns my personal experience in becoming a stage hypnotist. I put forth this information only for you to understand my perspective on the subject of hypnotism as entertainment.

No one was more skeptical of hypnotism than I was back in 1966 when I was invited to see a stage hypnosis show in Lawrence, Massachusetts at the Capri Restaurant. The hypnotist, Sam Vine, was breaking all attendance records putting subjects into hypnosis and having them perform like Hollywood stars every night of the week.

My first reaction to the invitation was, "No way! These shows are phony and the people onstage get paid to act silly." Little did I know how wrong I was and that my attendance at the show would actually lead me into a whole new career. Reluctantly, I went to the dinner show with my wife, Pat, and four other people, one of whom was a young girl in her twenties who was a very quiet and reserved person. After dinner and at the start of the show, I noticed that this young lady was no longer at our table but up on stage where Sam Vine very hastily had her dancing and singing like a professional actress! I was amazed, to say the least. How could this be? How could he take a very quiet, unassuming person and transform her into an outgoing actress giving a great performance? Well, from that time on, I was convinced that hypnosis was real, unrehearsed and the subjects were not paid to perform.

A few years later, I decided to take a hypnosis course and learn this craft. I became a pretty well-known stage hypnotist and had the wonderful opportunity of being featured on the TV show "20/20," being a headliner on cruise ships, including the beautiful QE2, and performing throughout the United States and the world in such arenas as London, Aruba, Jamaica, Puerto Rico, Dominican Republic, Mexico and more. Both Sam Vine and the "Dean of American Hypnotists," Ormond McGill, have had a most profound and positive effect on my career. Mr. McGill and I are currently teaching stage hypnosis together. It is my profound pleasure to be teaching with Mr. McGill, who has over 75 years of experience in the field of hypnosis.

Where is Stage Hypnosis Now?

Today, there is more interest in stage hypnosis shows than ever before. As a result, we have hundreds of stage hypnotists throughout the United States and Canada performing and delighting audiences nightly. This type of show has wide appeal because nothing is funnier than seeing your friends up on stage, perhaps revealing latent talent that they never knew they had. This is truly theater at its best.

This is what good, ethical stage hypnotists do. They elicit and direct volunteers to enter this wonderful state of relaxation whereby they become, mainly via their imaginations, fantastic entertainers.

Have you ever watched a dynamic stage hypnosis show and wondered if perhaps hypnosis might somehow improve your life in some capacity? When clean, ethical hypnotic demonstrations are presented, the hypnotist usually points out that in hypnotherapy, many people are able to make positive changes in their lives such as stopping smoking, weight control, stress control and many more self-improvement categories.

A professional stage hypnosis show is one of the funniest, most enjoyable experiences that you will ever watch or participate in. There is nothing funnier than seeing your friends perform on stage like Hollywood stars.

Many years ago, Art Linkletter had a show called "People Are Funny," and even without the use of hypnosis, Art would take people, dress them in some funny outfits and simply let them perform. It was just a hilarious show. It is amazing what people will do in the right situations and circumstances.

How Does It Actually Work?

When the subjects on stage enter a sufficient level of hypnosis, the hypnotist will select those that he/she feels are the best subjects and dismiss the others and return them to the audience. As the selected subjects enter the deeper levels of hypnosis the door to the subconscious mind opens and, while it give the subjects a "license to perform," very often talent just bursts from subjects who never knew they had it.

Once the volunteers are into what I call my "circle of concentration," nothing can disturb that hypnotic state. Most people do not realize that people in hypnosis can actually hear other sounds but they have the ability to "sink beneath" and ignore those sounds. When the show is over, the subjects actually feel just fantastic.

Have you ever wondered about participating in a stage hypnosis show? Have you wondered what it takes to be a good and receptive subject? I will tell you that it takes a little bit of concentration, willingness and lots of imagination. People with the most vivid imaginations usually make the best subjects. There also is an element of trust. Excellent hypnotists know that the most prized possession of a human being is a person's mind and when you volunteer to be hypnotized you are placing your trust in the hypnotist, and they should respect that and treat you with style and dignity.

If you have ever spoken to persons who have participated in a stage show, I can almost guarantee that they had a wonderful experience and felt absolutely marvelous and full of energy. This is because 15 minutes of a hypnotic sleep is equal to 2 or 3 hours of a regular sleep. That brings me to some common misconceptions.

Most Common Misconceptions

Q. People in hypnosis are sleeping.
A. Not true. Hypnosis is not actually sleep but a deep state of daydreaming.

Q. Someone can get stuck in hypnosis.
A. Has never happened. Since you have the power to remove yourself from hypnosis at anytime, you can never remain in hypnosis.

Q. Only weak-willed or stupid people can be hypnotized.
A. False! Over the last 34 years, I have hypnotized, on stage and privately, persons who are pilots, housewives, truck drivers, teachers, police, psychiatrists, professional athletes and more. The best subjects have good will power but just choose to follow the suggestions.

Q. People get embarrassed in hypnosis shows.
A. Yes, some do when the hypnotist's only goal is to get outrageous laughter from the audience with no regard to the person's welfare or dignity. I have done thousands of shows and have trained over 350 students to perform in the most ethical and dignified manner as possible. We value the trust given to us on stage.

Q. Hypnosis is dangerous.
A. Absolutely not true. Hypnosis has never been proven to cause any problem because it is simply a beautiful state of relaxation in which the subject is always and totally in control. Remember, the hypnotist does not force anyone to do anything against their will. He/she simply gets them to want to perform, and as far as the subjects are concerned, it is real.

As a stage hypnotist, I have had so much fun on stage that when people ask me what it is like to perform these shows, I tell them "I feel like a professional ball player getting paid to have fun. I get tremendous enjoyment by allowing people to be the stars of the show, so much so that very often I just break up laughing along with everyone else. Hypnosis on stage is really a fun venue where the audience actually laughs with the subjects on stage and not at them. That way, the subjects are very often open to volunteering again and perhaps those who did not volunteer might consider it next time.

Our goal, as ethical stage hypnotists, is to treat the subjects as we would like to be treated, leave them with wonderful feelings of relaxation and the thought that they did something that many have never experienced. And that is to give that audience, in this world of strife and violence, the opportunity for the 1-hour show to "laugh their heads off" and for that let's give them a thunderous round of applause!

In summation, I would like to leave you with a thirst to not only go to see a stage hypnosis show, but to perhaps actually volunteer and participate in it. Therefore, you will get a first-hand experience of precisely what it feels like and, who knows, you just might be the next Hollywood star with your very own walk of fame!

Jerry Valley, MACP; Valley Hypnosis, Inc. Methuen, MA has been a featured stage hypnotist on ABC-TV's "20/20". His career spans over 31 years and has given him the opportunity to appear all over the world as one of the finest entertainers in show business. Jerry has been the guest star on many television shows. Jerry is the recipient of the prestigious President's Award presented to him by the National Guild of Hypnotists.

Chapter 34
Hypnoanalysis

The term hypnoanalysis traces its roots to the original works of Freud, Jung and the other psychodynamically orientated founding fathers. Where hypnoanalysis differs from traditional psychodynamic psychotherapy is the speed in which hypnosis allows for a client to discover the root cause of their issue. This hypnotic process relies heavily on the use of hypnotic age regression. This is when a client, whilst in a hypnotic state, is taken back in time through the guidance of the hypnotist. By going back through the client's personal history it is possible for the client to gain insights into the genuine cause of their personal issues.

Similar to the Freudian theory, the assumption in hypnoanalysis is that difficulties generally can be traced back to the "imprinting phase" of development, which is considered to be the ages of 0-7. At this age, we have not developed the ability to see the world in other than a black and white way. By this I mean that a child does not have the cognitive ability to see that situations are not either good or bad, but are in fact, a shade of grey. Therefore a child may feel significant negative emotion in a situation which to an adult is either insignificant, or one that can be rationalized.

In this state, the "younger" client makes a decision at an unconscious level, which they take throughout their life. This means that even though the issue may not be obviously linked to the root cause, there are sufficient similarities that act as "reminders" to the client (unconsciously) as to how to react or behave. This reaction or behavior is often negative and unhelpful to the client.

Utilizing regression to go back and rationalize the root cause, using the client's adult mind, allows the past to be left in the past and enables the client to move forward with a sense of relief and resolution. This rationalization can take the form of simple understanding or emotional catharsis.

Hypnotists who practice hypnoanalysis sometimes identify themselves as "Hypno-Analysts," but simply put, these practitioners use regression to cause as their means of assisting clients to achieve their goals. It should be noted that hypnoanalysis might require several sessions to reach a successful resolution. The process is often a gradual one, as the unconscious mind develops a trust in the process. Part of this development can often be the exploration of one or more secondary events (which have compounded the original) before the process reaches the initial sensitizing event. Several schools of hypnotherapeutic thought incorporate hypnoanalysis without identifying it by that term.

Shaun Brookhouse, MA, PhD, CertEd, CI, FNGH, is the Director of Brookhouse Hypnotherapy Ltd, Principal of the Washington School of Clinical and Advanced Hypnosis and Director of Education of the UK Academy of Therapeutic Arts and Sciences in London, England. He can be contacted for hypnosis consultations or training at +44 161 881 1677
www.hypno-nlp.com or enquiries@hypno-manchester.co.uk

Chapter 35
Hypnotic Age Regression

Most hypnosis professionals agree that everything you have ever experienced, along with all of the meaning and emotions that you associated with the events of your life, are stored in your subconscious mind. When you are in hypnosis you can bring up this information and even relive those events from your past. As a result, hypnotic age regression is one of the most powerful tools available to the professional hypnotist or hypnotist to enable them to get long lasting results.

How Hypnotic Age Regression Works

The use of age regression can bring about success when many other efforts have failed. This is because when regression is used properly:

1. It can uncover the true cause of the problem (as well as events that reinforced it),
2. It can remove fears and misperceptions from the past that cause problems, and
3. It causes the subconscious mind to become more receptive to positive suggestions.

Hypnotic age regression provides you with insight into how and why a problem exists.

Without this kind of understanding, solutions to the problem may not address the real cause and may provide you with only temporary results or none at all. But when you experience hypnotic age regression you can actually revisit the cause of the problem, no matter where it may lie in your past. With the cause revealed, you and your hypnotist have a much greater understanding of how to deal with it.

Part of the magic of how age regression works can be understood by examining the expression, "I only wish I would have known then what I know now." With age regression you can, in a way, do just that. When you revisit this time in the past you can take what you know now to that event and see it with much greater understanding.

Take, for example, a problem which started when as a child an individual misunderstood a situation, such as receiving a stern word or two from a parent. As a child she may have thought that this meant that her parent did not love her or that there was something terribly wrong with her. Then when she revisits the situation in hypnosis she can understand the situation differently, seeing now that it was just a normal childhood mistake that led to the harsh words and that there was really nothing wrong with her. Furthermore, she could learn that the event did not cause her parents to stop loving her. This insight is brought to the child, completely rewriting the meanings associated with the incident that caused the problem.

Once an age regression has been conducted you are much more likely to accept hypnotic suggestions that are more in line with the truth about who you are and what you can accomplish in life. Gone will be the erroneous fears which started so many years ago, such as the fear of public speaking, fear of heights, fears of spiders or snakes and so on. Gone will be the limiting beliefs such as unworthiness or erroneous feelings such as guilt and fear.

Because hypnotic age regression is an insight-based approach to hypnosis, the insights that are gained are permanent. Any suggestions that are given to a client that are consistent with those insights can also be just as long lasting.

Hypnotherapists who use hypnotic age regression undergo special training, and not all hypnotherapists are qualified to use it.

Uses for Hypnotic Age Regression

Hypnotic age regression enables you and your hypnotherapist to quickly remove any issue that is based on fears or misperceptions of the past. These can include fears, limiting beliefs, bad habits and even psychosomatic illnesses. Other uses for hypnotic age regression include helping police departments to uncover details or evidence regarding a crime. Hypnotic age regression is also used to help find lost items.

Calvin D. Banyan, M.A., CH, BCH is a Board Certified Hypnotherapist and Certified Hypnotherapy Instructor and author of two books, Hypnosis and Hypnotherapy: Basic to Advanced Techniques for the Professional *(co-authored with Gerald F. Kein), and* The Secret Language of Feelings. *E-mail him at CalBanyan@HypnosisCenter.com or visit his web site at www.HypnosisCenter.com.*

Chapter 36
Past Lives:
Real or Imagined? It Really Doesn't Matter!

I can vividly remember the first time someone started talking past lives to me. I thought "what nonsense." I was taking my first hypnosis training and was grateful that past lives was not part of the curriculum. One of the other students keep telling me about her past lives with her husband and how it related to the difficult relationship they had in this life. They had been brother and sister before and he had killed her in that lifetime, and her story went on and on and on and on. I had heard all I wanted to hear in the first 30 seconds of our conversation. It was all I could do to keep from putting my hands over my ears, but I was brought up better than that. I simply wanted to learn about hypnosis and this sounded too farfetched to me.

But information on past lives just kept hitting me in the face. On a trip to our local library, a book on past lives "just happened" to be left on the table where I was sitting. I decided to check it out and see what all the nonsense was about. It was like checking out an X-rated book. I didn't want anyone to know what I was reading.

I can safely say that today my attitude has changed tremendously. Having learned so much about myself and seeing how recalling past lives has helped others makes it impossible not to embrace the fact that past life recall is an incredibly beneficial tool in helping us to understand ourselves more clearly. Whether these "memories" are real, or simply a figment of our imagination, really doesn't matter to me. The results are the same. So please keep an open mind as I relate a few of my favorite regressions.

Cat Allergy And Asthma: Gone!

Sue had called because she was interested in taking some hypnosis training. At the time I was looking for volunteer subjects for a class I was teaching and she agreed to come. Although we are usually looking for something simple, it sounded fascinating to have an opportunity to work on her cat allergy. I love a challenge! This sounded like a wonderful opportunity for my students to see how vast an area hypnosis covers.

We arranged to have one of the students induce hypnosis, then I would give a demonstration on age regression, back to when she had her first negative reaction to cats. First I got permission from her subconscious to go to the source of the problem. Sue immediately went into an asthmatic attack. Using a technique I call "The Silencer," I had her erase that memory and focus on music, while I talked to the deep inner unconscious mind. Permission was granted and I had her go back to 1 hour before the incident. Typically, in regression, we ask the subject to describe their feet, their clothing and their age. Sue said she was 5-years-old but as she described her clothing, I realized we were into a past life, not at all what I had expected. "Are you with someone?" I asked. She responded, "Yes, with the tribe." She was called "Little One" and was in India. She was now old enough to help her mother prepare lunch to take to the men working in the fields. This caused her a great deal of fear, as she had heard of tigers attacking people. You guessed it! Little One was attacked by a tiger and killed. We need to find the lesson when retrieving past lives and her lesson was that fear can bring about danger. Instantaneously, Sue had entered into another past-life. In fact it was the first time I had seen two past lives occur simultaneously. I needed to put the second one aside in order to complete the first one. This time she describe a bear clawing a hut to shreds and dragging her mother off. Her mother's body had been retrieved by the natives. When I asked, "Where are you?" she said, "In her belly." The natives cut the unborn child from her mother's womb and her father desperately tried to breathe life into his child. She saw the spirit of her mother and the infant going into the light. What could possibly have been a lesson from this life time? She described her parents as being elderly people who had thought they were unable to have children. They had been overjoyed with the prospect of this child coming into their lives. What she had learned from this life was a tremendous feeling of love.

Prior to the session Sue had described her asthma as being so bad it prevented her from staying outdoors in the winter more than 10 minutes without experiencing great difficulty with her breathing. She always had plenty of inhalers readily available. Shortly after this experience there had been such a severe snow storm in Chicago that thousands of homes and businesses were without electricity. Sue was able to be outside, shoveling no less, for an hour and a half.

Since then Sue no longer needs inhalers as her asthma is gone! As far as the cat allergies ... she now sleeps with the family cat!

Fear of Prosperity

This is a common thread that so many people have experienced, the inability to hold onto money. Her comment was, "I don't ever want to keep any money." Lynn was regressed back to a life time when her father was extremely wealthy. She had a beautiful large bedroom filled with toys. However, as Christine, a child of 4, she was extremely lonely, isolated from the other children she saw playing together in the village. Her father was distant and cold, and she was raised by servants. When she advanced to her death scene, she was a nun. She had "taken the vow of poverty" and her inheritance now belonged to the church, where it helped people in need.

Charlene Ackerman, CI, CH, has been teaching NGH certification classes since 1997 at The Wellness Training Center, a state approved school in Wisconsin. Her practice has expanded to Taiwan for counselors and physicians. She was given the honor of NGH Instructor of the Year 2000 and has previously been named NGH Member of the Year. She is author of numerous articles as well as books on hypnosis.

Chapter 37
Guided Imagery

Guided imagery is one of the finest tools in a hypnotist's resource bag for effecting positive results. Why? Because expert imagery speaks in the same rich language as the subconscious, and when we communicate with the subconscious, profound changes may be made.

We are actually all familiar with the language of the subconscious mind, for we are immersed in it nearly every night, in our dreams. The components of this language include symbolism, archetypes and/or metaphors which come into our dream awareness via the five senses.

The Five Senses

When we dream, our subconscious loves to engage us fully by painting colorful pictures, creating tangible textures, arousing our taste buds, proffering fragrances and throwing in a soundtrack to boot. When we speak back to the subconscious using guided imagery, we similarly want to involve as many as the five senses as possible. Expert hypnotists today recognize that this is the way in which we communicate with the subconscious most powerfully.

Many hypnotists used to practice guided visualization, instructing their clients to "see" mental pictures. One of the shortcomings of guided visualization was that it focused on only one sense, that of sight. Another was that it omitted a segment of the population. Some people cannot visualize at all, even though they are capable of experiencing inner journeys by using their other senses.

The term guided imagery, while imperfect, is more inclusive of these five senses, and is becoming the preferred term, replacing the limitations of the old phrase guided visualization.

Do this experiment:
* Picture a red barn on a farm. See it as clearly as possible.
* Now add to your picture the sound of cows mooing...
* Add the taste of fresh, creamy milk...
* Add the feelings of scratchy bales of hay and rough barn boards...
* And now add the smells of manure and alfalfa.

Notice how each added sense enhances and expands the image of the barn.

Symbolism, Archetypes and Metaphor

In dreams, the subconscious rarely speaks to us in a direct fashion to get its point across. Instead, it incorporates symbols, archetypes and metaphors. If you have been working hard and need rest, for instance, your dreams won't spell that out in clear, exact terms. Instead, you may dream of cows resting peacefully in a barn, and deduce that the image symbolizes your deep need to rest.

A skilled hypnotist—the guide in guided imagery—can ascertain which symbols, archetypes and metaphors best resonate with a client. The hypnotist then helps the client create a setting using the five senses, and weaves appropriate symbolism, metaphor and archetypes into the imagery. Hypnotic suggestions are readily accepted by the subconscious when they are offered in this way, for we are speaking to it in its own language.

Guided Imagery in Hypnosis Sessions

Uses of guided imagery in a hypnosis session are as unlimited as the hypnotist's or client's imagination, and may include:

* Taking a metaphorical journey or going on a quest;
* Inner exploration;
* Creating a symbol to represent a behavior, pain, relationship or emotion;
* Taking action to confront, remove, destroy or let go of something;
* Taking action to create a desired behavior, emotion, attitude, physical feeling;
* Establishing a special place;
* Receiving a gift or energy;
* Rehearsing success;
* and more!

Guided imagery can be incorporated into nearly every hypnosis session. It may be utilized by itself or in combination with other modalities, such as direct suggestion or parts therapy, as an incredibly powerful tool for assisting clients to achieve their goals.

Mary Elizabeth Raines, CI, is a Certified Hypnosis Instructor and author. E-mail her at info@laughingcherub.com. Information about her books and CDs can be found at www.laughingcherub.com.

Chapter 38
HypnoMassage

Definition

Defining hypnomassage (hypnosis massage) is as complex as trying to accurately define hypnosis. From the term alone, we deduce it is hypnosis blended with massage. But immediately a question arises—which science, which field of study claims this new entity? Is it massage with hypnosis added, or hypnosis with massage added?

An additional problem is the fact that there are varied and interchangeable terms in both arenas, often with the word therapy attached. Massage and massage therapy seem to suggest the same thing, but indeed do not always mean the same in the massage community. Massage refers to just the act of performing various strokes on the body, often interpreted as relaxation massage. Massage therapy, on the other hand, has gained a reputation for specific techniques on anatomy for empirically proven, medical results. So if we place hypnomassage under the auspices of massage, do we then deal with hypnomassage and hypnomassage therapy?

And if we place the modality in the school of hypnosis, the same question arises. There is hypnosis, as in producing trance phenomena and demonstrating it (e.g. stage hypnosis); and there is use of hypnosis for therapeutic value, or hypnotherapy, as so many like to call it.

If it seems the above splits vernacular hairs, I think it is important that we at least consider these label/definition questions, because they will have a great deal to bear on the future, the education, the legitimacy of the presently emerging tool, Hypnomassage.

Having said all this, I like to define hypnomassage, both as a bodyworker (a massage therapist who has tools beyond mere massage, but who does indeed do massage) and hypnotist/hypnotherapist/instructor as simply massage that uses hypnosis. The use can be either for relaxation/stress reduction or for therapeutic value. It really depends upon the client and the goal of the session. I believe there is great benefit to either and/or both goals. I also believe that bodywork in and of itself can be induction; and therefore massage itself can be termed a form of non-verbal hypnosis. Mixing this induction with further suggestion (see below) can be very powerful indeed.

Consideration

Given the general, accepting climate in the U.S. today for massage therapy, I would venture to say that it is much more legitimate for a licensed or certified massage therapist to perform hypnomassage than for a certified or licensed hypnotherapist. This is because the use of touch has remained very taboo within the latter field, for obvious and ethical reasons. It is true that various massage regulatory groups have suggested that massage "under" hypnosis is contraindicated because the client is not able to gauge the amount of pressure, perhaps resulting in injury. However, a competent hypnomassage practitioner would indeed counter the objection by making the irrefutable point that all hypnosis is self-hypnosis, and the individual enjoying hypnomassage is quite able to accept only beneficial touch, pressure and suggestions and would never allow such injury to occur.

In addition, there seem to be in most states and municipalities no specific laws and rules that prohibit the massage therapist from utilizing such things as suggestion, visualization, guided meditation and the like. This has been the case for some time, and for the past 10 years of being a Certified Instructor for the National Guild, a major portion of my students each year are massage therapists interested in merging the two careers.

Additionally, there is a new trend in massage legislation that gives hypnotists interested in doing bodywork/hypnomassage more than a glimmer of hope: the fact that energy workers are now being exempted from many such massage laws. In almost every case, state laws (31 of them regulating massage as of 2004) have defined massage therapy as "manipulation of soft tissue." Workers who touch the body but do not manipulate said tissue are now not placed under massage therapy restriction: Reiki therapists, polarity therapists, acupressurists, among others.

Therefore one might not have to have an actual credential in massage to enter the new and emerging field. We are now seeing combinations that describe their styles as "hypnotouch;" "hypnoacupressure," "hypnoreiki."

Returning to hypnomassage, however, it is essential that hypnomassage workers know the regulations in their state and/or municipalities, and seek out the proper massage licensure before going further in the public eye. Once this has been done, the territory, as we will see, is wide-open, unchartered, and very challenging.

Uses

As previously discussed, the use of hypnosis with bodywork/massage can run the gamut from general relaxation to a specific therapeutic goal. I have dealt with both for years, and, they are not mutually exclusive. Since massage can be, by itself, trance producing, relaxation is a major part. As induction tools, a worker might utilize soft music, soft lighting, soft voice. I often use breathwork to begin hypnomassage with suggestions like, "Take in a nice, long breath. Good. Another. Good. Another and hold it. Let it out slowly, easing out all tension, all worry, all muscle ache as you exhale." In fact, when I teach my own brand of metaphysical relaxation massage at my mountain (Bennington) center, I call it transformational—a pun, double entendre, for "Trance Formational." Thus we can use hypnomassage for any stress reduction purpose for which we would use hypnosis. It can be short with a few suggestions, or it can indeed run the course of the entire bodywork session. Doing the latter is always a treat for me, and often involves elaborate journeys inward with the client, perhaps suggesting a visit to the chakras to cleanse, balance and harmonize each one in turn. I might do the same with acupressure points, emphasizing the deep relaxation that each in a specific sequence can bring. Some of the sequences are ancient, coming from the bodywork of China: Tui Na.

On a more medical, therapeutic model, hypnomassage can be a wonderful asset to clients with clinical conditions.

After attempting to permeate trapezius (shoulder) muscles of a client without success, I have suggested on occasion that the client go inward, right to the muscle itself, to communicate with this muscle directly. What is the muscle trying to say?

Trying to tell the individual? Logically the muscle is there to serve the person. Why has it decided to give pain signals, almost without let-up, despite all attempts to soften it, to relieve its congestion? I recall vividly in one of my clients how the entire message became clear when in dialogue with the muscle. This female client was told by her trapezius that it was angry at how she literally took the weight of the world on her shoulders. As soon as she communicated that she understood this, despite the fact that her situation could not alleviate that burden entirely, the pain was all but gone! And I continued bodywork during this entire silent process, and could actually feel the tissue change. Even past life regression has been done under massage, with remarkable results. Some of these techniques of hypnomassage I developed 15 years ago while studying the psychology of illness with Dr. Bernie Seigel, who utilized similar techniques with cancer patients.

Future Trends

Because it can achieve results that massage or hypnosis alone may not, hypnomassage faces a promising future in the private and public sectors, as both an art and a science. If individuals in both fields continue to gain knowledge in the subject through research and experience, the current popularity of hypnosis and massage as separate entities will undoubtedly lead to a new, vigorous field—hypnomassage. And that entity will also undoubtedly gain the legitimacy that both fields have gained in turn. To those joining me and many, many others in this new mental, spiritual and physical tool: welcome!

Robert F. Adams holds a master's degree in human service administration from Antioch College and is a State of NH Licensed Massage Therapist; a certified acupressurist, hypnotist and breathworker; and a Reiki Master. He is a Certified Instructor for the National Guild of Hypnotists.

Chapter 39
Conversational Hypnosis

Conversational hypnosis is intentionally directing the mind of the person you are talking with to specific productive states of mind. That's a fancy way of saying that if someone is feeling something negative, bad or sad, you can use conversational hypnosis to literally move them from this stuck and unproductive state to a resourceful and positive state of mind.

This is done by using specific words, phrases, images and triggering previous conditioning in the person with or without them knowing you are doing so. Conversational hypnosis can be used to get the kids to help with chores, get your husband to cut the lawn and pay attention to you on Sunday afternoon or just about anything, including sales and marketing.

Someone who is particularly good at conversational hypnosis will be able to direct the thinking of almost anyone to productive states in a very, very short period of time.

Over the last few decades we have discovered that some words are simply keys to people's minds. Words like "now," "please", "imagine," "because," a person's name, "don't," literally open doors to people's minds.

Phrases like, "You probably are aware," "Some of the smartest ...," "The very best ...." and any phrase that presupposes knowledge of something, for example, will move the person to accept whatever comes next.

Many people use conversational hypnosis every day without even knowing it. And although it seems to work like magic (and it really does) it is something anyone can learn. Best of all, it's fun to do. There is something special about going around on purpose pushing buttons in other people's minds to program them (pardon the old metaphor) to have good feelings and thoughts.

When you learn the core skills of conversational hypnosis, which can be done in a few days of study, you can literally go through life finding ways to make people feel better, be happier and, even if it's just for the moment, change their life for the better.

Kevin Hogan, PsyD; Minneapolis Institute of Hypnosis and Hypnotheapy, Burnville, MN is the author of 10 books including The Psychology of Persuasion *and* The Science of Influence, Covert Hypnosis, The New Hypnotherapy Handbook *and the best selling* Irresistible Attraction. *He has acted as a consultant and is a sought after corporate trainer and speaker.*

Chapter 40
Subconscious Behavior Patterns

The conscious and subconscious minds are very different. The conscious mind is very analytical, while the subconscious mind takes everything literally. For example, suppose someone was walking down the street and a person came up to him and asked, "Do you know what time it is?" If the person was operating on a subconscious level, the response would be, "Yes." The inquirer would then ask, "Could you tell me what time it is?" Once again, the answer would be, "Yes." The inquirer would then ask, "What time is it?" The individual would then reveal the information that was requested.

If the inquirer came up to an individual who was working on a conscious level, the person with the watch would analyze, "Oh, this person is asking me what time it is, so either they don't have a watch, or theirs is broken. He can see that I have a watch on, so he knows that I have the information that he wants." As the person realizes what the other individual is asking, the person with the watch would immediately respond with the correct time.

As you can see, it would take three questions to get the same information as opposed to one. The subconscious mind takes everything literally. When asked, "Do you know what time it is?" Of course, you do! That is the question being asked, so the answer is given for that information only. The subconscious mind doesn't analyze the question as the conscious mind does, so it takes longer to get the needed information.

Here's another example. A woman is having a party. Her five-year-old daughter comes in and asks, "Mommy, can I have a piece of cake?" The mother says, "Yes." She cuts a piece of cake and has her daughter sit in the kitchen to eat it. A few minutes later the little girl comes up to her mother and says, "Mommy, I didn't like that cake." Her mother tells her to throw the cake away. Later, the woman goes into the kitchen to get the cake for her guests. She discovers that the cake is in the trash can! Well, she told her daughter to throw the cake away. She didn't say, "throw your piece of cake away." The small child didn't analyze what the mother said; she took it literally – just like our subconscious mind would do! So, our subconscious mind is like a five-year-old child. It does exactly what is asked; it doesn't read between the lines.

The subconscious mind is very fascinating. It is so simple, yet so complex. The subconscious mind is in control of all of our automatic functions and habits. Right now, are you thinking about making your heart beat? Of course not; it happens automatically through the subconscious mind.

Some research says that if you do an activity for 21 days in a row, it becomes a habit. The good thing about habits is that anything that can be learned can be re-learned. When a person has a habit of biting their fingernails, this is an automatic function; something that is controlled by the subconscious mind. It is not analyzed, "Oh, this fingernail is getting long enough to bite." The fingers move towards the mouth without any conscious thought.

Hypnosis is helpful in removing negative habits like nail biting. This habit serves no purpose. By giving positive suggestions to your subconscious mind to change your perception of nail biting, it is easy to eliminate this habit. Hypnosis works on the subconscious level. When positive suggestions are accepted, your goal is achieved.

Donald J. Mottin, FNGH, Mottin & Johnson, Bridgeton, MO, opened his first office in August 1980. Don has the practical experience in every phase of hypnosis. He was named the NGH Educator of the Year in 1993, 1996 and 2000. He has received numerous other awards.

Chapter 41
Bonus Book Excerpt

Are there actually secrets to self-hypnosis? Yes, inasmuch as in all probability you have no idea at all about how to experience self-hypnosis, and also what you will experience when you achieve that altered state of consciousness.

Just think of the the possibilities that lie in store for you when you learn to use the innate power of your subconscious mind to program your mind/body for positive mental and physical results—powerful self-confidence, a healthier mind and body, achievement of your personal goals. In other words, a better life, a more positive life, a life filled with love, happiness and all the good things you could desire.

In his book, Your Greatest Power, *author J. Martin Kohe taught that the greatest power a person has is the power to choose. In our experience we have found that that people don't know this and if they do know it they don't know how to use their greatest power—they don't know how to make the right choices for greater personal and professional success.*

As the co-authors of the book HypnoMotivation® *we know how to use their greatest power, the power to choose, and best of all, we also have the key ingredient that will allow anybody to get the most out of this power for themselves. If you are ready to make positive choices in your life we are ready to teach you how to unleash the power of self-hypnosis using what we call hypnomotivation.*

In our book we give you case studies and examples of how others have utilized hypnomotivation, sometimes knowingly, and sometimes not even realizing it as they enjoy the wonderful, positive benefits that happen in their lives. We both know from personal experience how hypnomotivation, intensified with self-hypnosis will get you through the tough spots in life, the real-life soap operas, the fears, apprehensions, anxieties, nervousness, the love and the grief that all are a natural part of living.

Are we promising you a perfect life without any of the negatives or trials and tribulations? That would be truly wonderful, but I'm afraid that isn't the case. What we do want to teach you is how to be prepared and how to overcome all of the aforementioned problems so that they simply become challenges rather than obstacles. We are including the first lesson presented in HypnoMotivation® *as a bonus to readers of* The Official Consumer Guide to Hypnotism. *This lesson and all of the others in the book can be used by anyone just as presented here, however, they are greatly enhanced when combined with self-hypnosis . . . thus, the term "hypnomotivation."*

SUCCESS IS A JOURNEY NOT A DESTINATION

"I will not wait to become a successful person ... someday.
I AM a successful person NOW.
It is my concentration on and devotion to being successful each and every day that will let me achieve my future goal."

Success is a tantalizing word: people do not agree on what it means to them. How about you? In circles where a person is valued for his money and deferred to for it, success means personal property, more money, a bigger home, travel abroad, boats, cars, swimming pools, and leisure. Or is success to you a status symbol that compels the admiration of family, friends and neighbors? Perhaps success means the big escape from fear, frustration, debts, mediocrity, and failure. Actually these are only by-products of real success. You attain your ambition: you reach your goal, and the rest follows.

Why shouldn't everyone want to be a success? It is surprising, but sadly true. Look around you today and what do you often find? A stifling, negative atmosphere fostered by mediocrity. Many times our teachers are those who bombarded us with failure messages, with so much negativity that we don't even realize that success is easily possible for us.

Is *your* thinking wrong? It could be. Why don't we travel on the Success Superhighway instead of the rutted back road of banality?

Success is a journey, not a destination. Go first class. Get on the superhighway. It doesn't cost a penny more than overcrowded secondary roads.

Believe in yourself. Believe you can travel first class and you will! When you have confidence in yourself, others will, too. "I'll give it a try ... BUT ..." is a poor risk attitude because you doubt and you disbelieve in yourself. These are powerful negatives that will hold you down.

Actually, not wanting to succeed is the reason so many men and women fail. Figure it out. As a person becomes more successful, more responsibility must be assumed, and this is what holds many back. Even more, those who control today's opinion machinery, have so brainwashed us with negative ideas that many people don't want to succeed. They believe they never will; it could upset accepted ideas if they did succeed!

Attitude is the number one factor in success. Make that critical decision to succeed now, and you *are* a success, right now. You changed your attitude from a Failure Syndrome to a Success Complex. You have other steps to take, but first of all, you must make the decision to drop a negative life that is as genuine as Zirconian diamonds. You must adopt the positive attitude toward life.

Everything does not turn out 100% when you make this decision. There will still be negative situations and setbacks, now and then, but you will learn how to handle them as you speed along the Success Superhighway. Expect to lose an occasional battle and win the war.

Most of us have hypnotized ourselves with negative ideas. That's why we start the day with a poor attitude that grows progressively worse as the day goes on. Success is *now*, not what we will become some day in our dreams. It is what we are! Actually your idea of success determines your success. If you are thinking of a far off goal, you can confuse accomplishment with success. You may be a millionaire ten years from now, but no more of a success than you are this very minute. All you accomplished is the goal of a million dollars, which doesn't make you a success. It is a journey, not a destination. You must be a success *now*. On your life journey, you succeed in various accomplishments such as becoming a millionaire.

Are you a good investment to others? Would you be a good investment for a bank, a loan department, or for that matter, anyone to spend time, effort, or money on? If so, start by investing in yourself. Concentration, singlemindedness of purpose, and the establishment of a specific plan are the best initial investments you can make in your successful journey through life.

What is success to you? Don't you in your heart believe that the person who is happy, dedicated and determined at working to the best of his or her ability is a success? That individual could be the best darn anything in the world, whistling and smiling and taking pride in the job or profession provided he has an income that will take care of his obligations.

You know, you are a success *now*, or you wouldn't be sitting here, reading this book. Whether you will be a success an hour, a day, or a week from now depends on you. Make up your mind. make your decision and then act towards a more successful life. You must become success conscious. You develop the correct attitude. Only then, you get from life what you put into it.

So it takes 100% effort to achieve 100% results.

Steps to take:

1. MAKE A DECISION. ("I am a successful person right now.")

2. TAKE AN ACTION STEP. (List all the positive attributes you now possess.)

3. PLAN YOUR WORK. (List your daily, weekly, monthly and yearly goals. Also list any negative attributes you now possess & plan to change or eliminate.)

4. WORK YOUR PLAN. (Start to accomplish the goals and change the negatives in step 3.)

Dwight F. Damon, DC, DNGH, OB, is President of the National Guild of Hypnotists, Inc. and a founding member. He is Editor of The Journal of Hypnotism®, *the* Hypno-Gram®, *and* Hypnosis Today®. *He has been a consultant on hypnotism for the* Readers Digest Guide to Natural Health *and other national and international media projects.*

Dr. Damon started his career as a student and associate of Dr. Rexford L. North, and is the author of several books in the fields of motivation and magic. He has maintained careers as a Doctor of Chiropractic, TV personality, motivational teacher, and theatrical entrepreneur. He was named Citizen of the Year twice, and was appointed as "New Hampshire's Magical Goodwill Ambassador" by NH Governor Meldrim Thomson, Jr.

Patricia E. MacIsaac, LPN, FNGH, CMI, OB, is the owner of the South Shore Hypnosis Center in Hingham, MA, and is a frequent lecturer and facilitator of workshops and seminars. She is certified to teach all NGH training courses, and is the recipient of the NGH Meritorious Service Award in 1993, Certified Instructor of the Year in 1995, Hypnotism Hallmark Award in 2006, and the Dr. Rexford L. North Award in 2007. She was also featured twice on the cover of the Journal of Hypnotism, *and is a member of the NGH Board of Examiners, Advisory Board, President's Cabinet, and Board of Directors of NFH local 104.*

Patricia has taught, and applied the art and science of hypnotism to groups and individuals nationally and internationally.

Chapter 42
The Innovations of Hypnosis

We can read much about hypnosis and realize that it is a viable tool to achieve many goals, but what do we really know of hypnosis when it comes to hypnotizing a difficult person? Are you a difficult person to hypnotize?

Hypnosis is one of those special arts that has found new ground. However, much of society still has the view that hypnotists swing watches in front of the eyes of their subjects or clients. There are so many techniques that are currently used in today's world to hypnotize a person that no one is left behind. Sigmund Freud made a statement once that said, "Only the deepest of subjects can benefit from hypnosis!" For many years following that statement, hypnotists followed that philosophy.

Actually, hypnosis not only has gone through a great rehabilitation of new and improved techniques for the most difficult of subjects or clients, but modern technology has been incorporated by people that have never been hypnotized by learning self-hypnosis and by using tapes or CDs for self-improvement. Even biofeedback techniques have been used for many years to teach people how to relax well by having electronic instrumentation feed signals back to them when they have achieved the relaxation that is sufficient for them to relax well.

Being hypnotized by any method is a great adventure for most people, except for the few that attempt to intellectualize or resist the process. These, of course, have always been called "difficult subjects!" With the technology of today in audio and the skills of the average hypnotist, almost anyone can be hypnotized easily. Contrary to popular beliefs, anyone can be hypnotized easily and at times for some, even more effectively using electronics to aid in this relaxation. I personally use recordings to induce a deeper or more profound level of hypnosis for the person who resists hypnosis. When I hypnotize an individual, I hypnotize them while they are seated in a separate room wearing headphones and I speak to them through microphones while they listen wearing special headphones made by Bose to shut out any background noise. I personally feel that the less excuses an individual has not to respond, the better the results will be. These excuses are not irrational. Many people truly do have difficulty surrendering or relaxing in a situation when they might feel vulnerable. Imagine your first experience with hypnosis and the hypnotist is next to you as you are sitting there with your eyes closed and attempting to relax. It is not an easy situation for some people seeking hypnosis as a method of improving their lives. Too often, I have heard, "I tried hypnosis and it didn't work!"

I could cringe when I hear that phrase, as it sends a message to many that if they attempted hypnosis and it didn't work, then they most likely could not benefit from hypnosis. That could not be further from the truth. I feel that even for the most difficult client, there is a method. In my situation, I have chosen to use the electronics described above to enhance their ability to be hypnotized. The most difficult person cannot fight the power of objectivity with a recording made during the ultimate level of the skills of the hypnotist. Traditional hypnosis works well for most individuals, but occasionally that difficult person comes along and then a separate room, wearing headphones with the addition of selected recordings made at the ultimate skills of the hypnotist will remove potential failure from almost anyone. This is a method designed for the most challenging individual.

Even the idea of using a tape or CD to learn self-hypnosis can add to your success. Imagine finding the right voice, the right technique and combine that with the privacy of your own home. That would be the ultimate of success. Who knows your mind and the ability to relax better than you? Since the theory is that all hypnosis is self-hypnosis, then your own skills can accomplish the most in this situation. I feel that a self-hypnosis recording that is made well and used when you are in the best of moods to be hypnotized can assist many who have not accomplished hypnosis in a traditional method. I feel also that a recording can be personalized with your attitude while listening to it. If you have a recording that you relate to and relax well with, try this technique to enhance your success. When you lie back to start your self-hypnosis, begin to think of your goal as though you have already achieved it. This means create an "intent" as though it has been accomplished. We use intents in everyday life and never realize that intent is the magic of the mind in accomplishing your goal. Sure, positive thinking is good, repetitive suggestions can help, but when you lie back and feel as though you have already accomplished your goal, then you will have greater success.

Have you ever wanted a new living space and you went to look at a place that you really liked? You began to walk around and speak of how you would design each room, where things would go and what colors you would choose. You began to create intent. It is called "intent to purchase." It is a very legal and often binding issue, because you have given all of your consciousness to the purchase of this property. The word "intent" is a very powerful word and if you can learn to use intent well with a self-hypnosis recording, anything can be possible.

So you see, you can accomplish most anything using hypnosis, even if you think that you can't be hypnotized. Just incorporate some technology that is available and begin to find new skills available to you through your subconscious mind.

Larry Garrett, Garrett Wellness Center, Chicago, IL, has been doing hypnosis as a full time practice since 1970. He works with referrals from many physicians in the Chicago area and for the past 25 years worked with over 20 different police departments in the Chicago area.

Chapter 43
Cancer Patients and Hypnotism

Having cancer is scary. According to the American Cancer Society, most people who are diagnosed with cancer will survive it. Still, the diagnosis of cancer is something most people dread.

In the many years I have worked with cancer patients as a hypnotist I find as many people fear the treatment we have for cancer as fear the disease itself. While chemotherapy, radiation and surgery have become much less painful and disruptive than they were years ago, if you are a cancer patient the treatment that makes you well can also make you feel miserable.

Fortunately, hypnotism can help. A properly trained hypnotist working with the approval of your physician can dramatically improve the course of your treatment. Most of the side-effects of chemotherapy, including nausea, fatigue and discomfort can be soothed away by hypnotic suggestion. Pain can be reduced and the effectiveness of pain medication can be increased through hypnotism. Your appetite can be improved so that your body is able to receive the nutrition it needs to rebuild itself with healthy tissue, and your mood can be elevated so that you enjoy your life during the time you are a patient.

In addition to improving your quality of life, there is evidence that receiving hypnotism from a properly-trained practitioner can help you medically. In the ten-year outcomes study done on cancer patients at my hospital clinic we found that patients receiving hypnotic interventions had improved survival. While research on this is controversial, it is not hard to imagine why people who feel better, eat better, sleep better and who are more optimistic also live longer.

Many hospitals and wellness centers offer some form of support group for persons living with cancer, often including guided imagery or visualization for health. While these programs are valuable, they should not be confused with professional hypnotism.

Guided imagery and visualization form only a small and relatively minor part of the skill set of a properly trained and certified hypnotist. Your hypnotist has many more techniques and procedures that can be used to help a person living with cancer than even the most skilled visualization consultant. While imagery and visualization unquestionably help, most cancer patients will want to use the more extensive and powerful skills of the professional hypnotist.

If you decide to seek assistance from a hypnotic practitioner I strongly urge you to consider a professional who is trained and certified by the National Guild of Hypnotists. As the oldest and largest hypnosis organization in the world it holds its member to a high standard of ethics and professionalism. While few states license hypnotism, the certification of the National Guild of Hypnotists can always be trusted.

In order to work with you, a Guild certified hypnotist will require a referral from your physician. As there is mounting evidence in professional journals that hypnotism can be an effective adjunct in cancer care, your physician will almost certainly issue a referral on your request. In fact, you may discover that your oncologist has a list of practitioners that he or she recommends.

The Rev. C. Scot Giles is a Doctor of Ministry, a Board Certified Chaplain and a Fellow of the National Guild of Hypnotists. He directs the first hospital-based, medically approved program in America for the hypnotic treatment of cancer and is the author of the National Guild of Hypnotists curriculum in Complementary Medical Hypnotism. His web site is http://www.counselingministries.org and can be reached at CSGiles@uuma.org.

Chapter 44
Developing ESP with Hypnosis

For 33 years, I have enjoyed the positive, joyous excitement of using ESP in my daily life, as well as professionally. In fine tuning my courses over the years, I have found that by combining lectures, NLP, and my own version of creative imagery, people can become psychics on a positive and uplifting level. I have also found that this process can be greatly accelerated through the use of hypnosis. Using these techniques, my students have been able to function psychically, and with practice have gone on to become professional psychics and/or hypnotists.

As a trained psychic, I was chosen one of the top 10 psychics in the world two years in a row, due to the predictions I have made during the years which have come to pass. Intuition is the most positive, normal, healthy and rewarding sense you can develop to help yourself and others. By sensing what can happen in the present and the future, you can change what is negative and prevent much unnecessary unhappiness.

Every day of your life, you receive various promptings from within, whether it is for inventions, ideas for better health or artistic creations. These ideas usually come when you are in a state of self-hypnosis, commonly referred to as daydreaming. The resources of the mind are limitless, and can begin to flow when prompted by questions such as, "How can I help ...?" or "What would be necessary for the betterment of ...?" Each day I take a few moments to ask myself these and other questions. I do this in a state of self-hypnosis, meditation, prayer and conscious, controlled conversations with my Creator, my God, my Good.

One of the students I trained has been one of the most important gifts that God gave me. In July of last year, Marlene Monnar had a premonition, listened and acted on what she received intuitively. She rushed me to the hospital, where they ran a blood test and found out I was severely anemic and had a bleeding aneurism in my stomach which I did not know about. I was told I was near death. After being in the hospital for a week, and four surgeries later, the bleeding stopped. I was able to make it to the conference and teach my two workshops.

Using this type of hypnosis (yes, this is an evolved hypnotic technique) I created the ESP development game, Crystal Insights. This game was developed to help people recognize and use their own intuitive abilities. When I teach the use of the game in my ESP development class, I also use hypnotic conditioning cycles to impress the information contained in the manual for improved recall. I train the psychics to enter altered states to enhance their psychic ability, clear their minds and obtain more accurate information.

Ramona Garcia, The Open Door, Salem, NH is a respected National and International Psychic, Hypnotist and entertainer who lectures on parapsychology, success motivation, faith healing, hypnosis and the powers of the subconscious mind. Ramona teaches Hypnosis and NLP for phobias, stress management, developing your intuition, developing your artistic talents in art, music and writing, learning motivation and more.

Chapter 45
Parts Hypnosis

Have you ever tried to lose weight or quit smoking, only to find your subconscious resisting your attempts to change habits?

Hypnosis helps millions of people to achieve goals; yet, in spite of the best efforts of both client and therapist, unresolved inner conflicts often inhibit successful results. When other techniques fail, parts hypnosis often provides the key to success.

Parts hypnosis is based on the concept that our personality is composed of a number of various parts. Our personality parts are aspects of the subconscious, each with their respective jobs or functions of the inner mind. In other words, we wear many hats as we walk through the path of life.

The Hats We Wear

We are often aware of the various hats we wear from day to day. I wear my professional hat at work; but my inner child can't wait to come out and play when the workday ends.

Let's take this one step further. People wishing to overcome an undesired habit often seek professional help because a part of the mind blocks success. For example, a smoker might make a New Year's resolution to quit, only to find that resolution literally going up in smoke.

The dieter who avoids junk food at a social event goes out of control later at home, even after investing hundreds (or thousands) of dollars for a professional weight control program. It's as if another part of the personality takes over. These inner conflicts are common, and they occur when we have two different parts of the subconscious pulling us in opposite directions.

What Is Parts Hypnosis?

Parts hypnosis is the process of calling out and communicating directly with these parts of the subconscious. A deep state of hypnosis improves the results by reducing the risk of analytical resistance from the conscious mind.

The late Charles Tebbetts promoted and taught parts hypnosis because of its value in helping people resolve inner conflicts. Originally borrowing it from Paul Federn, Tebbetts evolved parts hypnosis into a client-centered approach to help people resolve inner conflicts. Most sessions involve calling out only the two parts in conflict, but other parts do exist.

Increasing numbers of therapists around the world are discovering the benefits of parts hypnosis and its variations to help clients get past personal barriers. (Variations are called: ego state hypnosis, submodalities, subpersonalities, voice dialogue, etc.) Regardless of the label, I believe this complex technique is the most beneficial hypnotic technique available for helping clients resolve inner conflicts.

Is Parts Hypnosis for You?

If you have ever been unable to overcome an undesired habit even after the use of hypnosis, you are probably a candidate for parts hypnosis. Also, even if you have never experienced hypnosis, parts hypnosis is worthy of consideration if you feel an inner conflict regarding your goal. Inner conflicts are present when you feel a strong desire to achieve a goal, yet you occasionally (or frequently) undermine your best efforts.

Often smokers, after failing to respond to traditional hypnosis, can finally attain inner resolution through parts hypnosis. Likewise, numerous clients attempting to control eating habits often gain important insight about themselves after experiencing hypnotic inner conflict resolution. Other inner conflicts can also be resolved with client-centered parts hypnosis.

Additionally, because a deeper hypnotic state increases the probability of lasting success, it is my professional opinion that a client will be best served by choosing a facilitator who is competently trained in both parts hypnosis and the art of hypnohypnosis.

Roy Hunter, Certified Hypnotism Instructor, is the published author of several highly respected books. Email him at [alliance@self-empowerment.tv].
Visit Roy's website at: www.royhunter.com

Chapter 46
What is NLP?

NLP is a unique model of how people learn, motivate themselves, and change their behavior to achieve excellence in any endeavor.
What does the term Neuro-Linguistic Programming mean?
NLP is an integration of Neurology, psychology, linguistics, cybernetics, and systems theory. It is Hypnosis with or without the trance.
Neuro, because our experiences, both conscious and subconscious, are derived through and from our senses and central nervous system.
Linguistic, because our mental processes are also coded, organized, given meaning and transformed through language
Programming = because people interact as a system in which experience and communication is composed of sequences of patterns or "programs."

NLP:
Lets you model or copy human excellence.
Can help you become adept in whatever you want to do.
Can change the impact of the past on a client.
Can change a poor speller to a good speller.
Can assist a business person to gain rapport nonverbally and run meetings efficiently.
Can help an athlete improve concentration.
Most therapy is remedial, meaning it is directed towards solving problems of the past.
NLP studies excellence and teaches the skills that promote positive changes that generate new possibilities and opportunities.
It is a process of teaching people to use their brains.

Here is an example of NLP in action:
Have you ever seen someone at a restaurant, trying to decide what they are going to order? They may look up, pause, look down, lick their lips, touch their stomach, then order something; or they may repeat the options to themselves (in their heads, or sometimes out loud, "a quarter pounder with cheese, hmm"). They may even ask someone else, "What's good?" (Hoping your tastes are similar.) Whatever they do, they are running some type of strategy, and most, if not all, of it is preconscious. We are not aware of how we do it. We just do it.

Psychology tells us that it is a learned behavior, which it is. But once learned, it is put out of our conscious awareness. Even a Pavlovian response can be considered a learned strategy. Think about the classical Pavlov training. A dog is presented with food, paired with a bell, repeatedly, until the bell alone will elicit a saliva response in the dog. Somewhere in that dog's brain, it is learning, Bell = food = eat or food = bell = eat. So it is with humans. We learn a strategy and then we use it over and over again, until we replace it or change it.

To make this easy to learn, think about what you ate the last time you went to a restaurant. How did you decide what to have? Did you look at the menu (visual), then mentally taste the food (gustatory, or kinesthetic)? Possibly you said something to yourself (auditory), when you found something you wished to order. Then you exited the program. (One reason it is hard for some people to order food when they are really hungry is that they get stuck in the program, and keep playing options: that sounds good, that looks good, I always liked that…..etc.)

You have strategies for everything you do, and a lot of them overlap. You may use the same style of strategy in different contexts. This may, or may not be problematic. I worked with a man who used his business strategy (which made him rich) to find a wife. He found his prospect (business venture), did his research (dating), found he wanted to acquire this property, and was willing to pay the asking rate (marriage). So they got married. He then took a hands off approach: paid the price, bought the house and cars. Now he was basically ignoring his wife, unless there was a problem (the way he would run a business). He needed a romantic strategy. The good part is you can change, install, or remove a strategy. This is one of the things we do with hypnotic suggestions.

Every person has their own strategy for everything they do. They will use these strategies when they communicate. These strategies are the primary (or lead), secondary, and tertiary representational systems of the person. For example a person can use a visual, auditory, or Kinesthetic strategy for buying a car. See a car you really like, hear good things about the car, drive the car and it feels good; buy the car, then rationalize the costs.

The following example is how I used strategies in a clinical setting. I had a client with whom I had been using hypnosis as a form of therapy. The client had tried hypnosis in the past for weight loss with limited success. Now she was stuck. She would do very well at work and through the main part of the day. She would have a small piece of fruit in the morning, a light lunch, if she was hungry, or she would walk, and not stop after work for a snack. She was making notable progress. She would, however, start eating at night and would overeat. Since she had done hypnosis and had some success, I thought we would see what her strategy was for eating at night.

She relaxed and I asked her what happened when she got home. At first she just said, "It seems like I walk in and start eating."

I *asked, "Tell me what happens as you walk inside the doorway of your home."*
"Well, I open the door and I see an empty apartment." She was divorced, and her youngest was in college. "Then what?" I prompted.
"I hear a voice that says a woman is not suppose to be alone."
"Whose voice?" I asked.
"My mother's."
"Then what happens?" I countered.
"I feel bad, like a little girl, a bad little girl," she replied softly.
"Then what?" I asked.
"I hear another voice and it says, Eat Something. You'll feel better." (Her mother again.)
"Then what do you do?" I prompted.
"I eat something, and I feel a little better. Then I feel guilty because I'm trying to lose weight ."
"Anything else?" I ask.
"I hear her voice again. 'Eat Something. You'll feel better.'" And so she was off on a binge.

The technique I decided to use was to bypass the whole mess, using hypnosis. While in trance she imagined that when she was opening the door she would say to herself that it was so nice to choose to live alone. She also would make plans to do things she had put off for years, dance class, movies, etc.

We could have spent years looking at the cause, but if we use hypnosis and NLP to change the behavior first, we remove the emotional charge. Then we can readjust the program. When hypnosis and NLP are combined it is one of the most powerful modalities known.

William D. Horton is a licensed psychologist, alcohol and drug counselor, master board certified hypnotist, and the worlds leading expert in NLP and hypnosis. He has taught all over the world and written several books. He founded the National Federation of Neuro Linguistic Programming In Florida. He can be contacted at 941-697-91041 or nfnlp@aol.com. Check his web site at nfnlp.com.

Chapter 47
Past Life Regression
Healing the Future by Exploring the Past

Is there a future in healing the past? Can we truly heal our lives by simply discovering past energies that might be holding us back? Absolutely. Past life regression work is a safe, comfortable, and wonderfully rewarding way to bring all aspects of our soul "selves" together, providing a complete wholeness in healing.

Past life memories are stored away in the attic of our unconsciousness like grandma's old lace doilies. These memories are the keys to the doors of all our experiences since we became souls, and hypnosis is a key to unlocking these memories. Perhaps you have, at one time or another, met someone for the first time and felt an immediate closeness, as if you were old friends. Perhaps you have traveled to a new place, only to find it was so innately familiar that you felt immediately at home. These are common experiences. Utilizing hypnotherapy, specifically past-life regression techniques, we are able to make sense of these experiences.

Past life regression is a beautiful, compassionate, and effective therapy that brings forth a new manner of healing that can be experienced when all of the body's energies are gathered together for a common goal. It is a relaxing, soothing, calm state of heightened awareness. The body feels restful and at peace, while the mind is acutely aware of each event that is occurring. This amazing journey into our own consciousness allows us to open the door to our soul's history, discovering information that may bring phenomenal change to our lives. We learn many things about ourselves, both from our present life experiences and from past incarnations. We gain insight into our current life by reviewing past experiences and mistakes.

The knowledge of our past hurts is balanced by the love and graciousness of the gifts we rediscover; gifts such as lost or forgotten skills or talents, soul memories or contacts. These gifts are brought forward and incorporated into the current life cycle, bringing a new wholeness to healing.

Some question whether the retrieval of past life memories is authentic. Does it work? Yes, and often with miraculous results. I have worked with many people and have found that everyone experiences regression differently. Children, especially the very young, have relatively clear memories of their past lives. The one thing that everyone has in common is that the regression experiences are not what they would have expected.

Hypnosis/past-life regression sessions are memorable and hypnosis is the doorway to deeply stored memory banks. It provides a method for exploring inner space in the mind and the uncharted sanctuary of the deeper self. The hypnotist simply assists the client in drawing out that which already exists. Through hypnosis, people are able to fit together the pieces of a puzzling past. When a past problem enters conscious awareness, it can be encountered honestly and then neutralized. When a pattern is changed, the problem is resolved.

Henry Leo Bolduc is Board Certified in hypnotism and past-life regression therapy. He has 42 years of experience in past-life regression and is the author of five books and hundreds of articles. He is a contributing columnist to the Journal of Hypnotism™. *Please visit his web sites at www.henrybolduc.com and www.creativespirit.net/henrybolduc*

Chapter 48
Dreams & Hypnotism

Many people may wonder how dreams and hypnotism work together. The common denominator is the subconscious mind.

In dreams the subconscious mind communicates with the conscious mind to give guidance, warnings, messages and information. There are times when we are so busy during our daily lives that we may not be aware of something in our lives that we need to know. Information comes to us as we sleep in our dreams so that we are able to receive these messages.

Hypnotism is relaxing and keeping an open mind to receive suggestions, either delivered by another person or given by yourself, to help you to reach your goals. When a person is hypnotized, they are awake. They can hear everything, and are aware of what is occurring. The person who is hypnotized is always in control. They cannot be made to do anything against their will.

When you combine these two techniques, remarkable results may occur. During the hypnosis session, suggestions may be given that prompt your dreams to give you needed information to achieve your goals.

We had a client who had lost her wallet. Her son needed medical attention, but her insurance card was in the wallet. She was desperate to find it. The last place that she remembered having it was at her friend's house. During hypnosis, we gave her the suggestion that she might remember where it was either immediately after the hypnosis session, or when she walked into the front door of her home. She would get the information she needed in her dreams and would know where the wallet was when she woke up in the morning. She called us the next day to say that she found the wallet when she woke up that morning. She walked over to her closet and found the wallet on the floor in one of her shoes. By combining these two powerful tools she was able to relax her mind and find the wallet so that her son received the help that he needed.

Another woman had a dream that her chest of drawers was broken. Then in the dream, she realized that the piece of furniture belonged to her husband. When she asked what the dream could mean, we asked her if her husband had any respiratory problems. She looked surprised and said that he had just told her that morning that he was going to stop smoking because he was having trouble breathing. Hypnosis then helped him to eliminate the smoking habit.

The mind is like a powerful magnet. Whatever you focus on, you are putting energy into and you draw it into your life. Since it takes just as much energy to focus on what you want as it does on what you don't want, why not put your thoughts and energy into what you want to occur in your life?

By learning how to program and interpret your dreams, you can reach your goals more easily. When incorporated with hypnosis, positive suggestions can be given to you that assist in this process. Your subconscious mind can be your best friend or your worst enemy. Use the powers that you possess so that you can be the very best that you can be.

Sweet dreams!

Bree Ferrario, CH, has interpreted dreams since 1975. She incorporated hypnosis with her dream work in 1995 to assist individuals in reaching their goals. You may reach Bree at her email address: hypnobree@msn.com

Chapter 49
Spirituality and Hypnotherapy

Hypnotherapy helps you to get in touch with your spiritual core. Because it's so relaxing, hypnotherapy quiets your mind enough for you to go deeply into your innermost self where there are profound treasures. Some people are astounded at the love they feel. Others find that the great wisdom there is guiding them to resolve their most difficult issues. Still others feel safe and protected, as if a blanket of peace and inner light had been wrapped around them. Hypnotherapy is akin to meditation and prayer, and many people report that they experience the force of life itself when they're in the relaxed state. The experience is non-denominational, and yet people are able to contact their own type of spirituality while in hypnosis. Some have experiences of Jesus. Others find the Buddha or Moses or Allah. Some find that they're in touch with inner guides or angels. All of these experiences are rich with value and healing power.

The Spirit of Healing

When you're able to contact this part of yourself, great healing is possible. People find they can move from their darkest inner states into the light when they make this connection. Fears fall away, anger turns into compassion, unwanted habits are released, pain lifts off, old difficult traumas are transformed. Everyone has the capacity to make these shifts, as everyone has been given the inner spiritual remedies as their inalienable rights. Even skeptics have found that during hypnotherapy they find a part of themselves that lifts them to a level of spiritual experience that changes their lives.

How This is Done

When hypnosis is induced, you become deeply relaxed. The depth of this relaxation varies from extremely deep to very light. Most people are in the middle of this continuum. No matter what the depth of your relaxation may be, the very act of relaxing takes you to a focused state within. Because there are no distractions, you are able to get in touch with your subconscious or deep inner mind, the repository of all that has taken place in your life. You're also able to get in touch with your superconscious mind, the place within you that is centered and whole and filled with healing power. This is a natural ability, which is enhanced by hypnosis. It helps you to contact this superconscious or higher mind because it is rich with inner remedies. It's a natural remedy of the soul.

A Deep Spiritual Experience

A man named Joseph had very low self-esteem. In fact, he thought he was terribly ugly. As he relaxed into hypnotherapy, he first experienced some darkness in his heart center. As he paid attention to it and watched it from within, the darkness began to move away, and a light emerged from within him. He then felt love for himself pouring through him, and he realized his own beauty as a fountain that came from inside. He knew that the reason he was experiencing this in his life was because he needed to wake up – and that he did!

A Vehicle for Transformation

Some people receive practical guidance in hypnotherapy. Others find more esoteric parts of themselves. It's a superb vehicle for personal transformation, and therefore it's a way to also make powerful changes in the quality of our world. It's through these shifts in consciousness that our world can hope to be transformed.

Marilyn Gordon, CH, CI, DCH, Center for Hypnotherapy Certification, Oakland, CA - is a certified hypnotherapist, certified Guild instructor, healer, teacher, speaker and author. She is the author of Extraordinary Healing: Transforming Your Consciousness, Your Energy System and Your Life. *She has been awarded the Hypnosis Achievement Award, the Charles Tebbetts Award for "Spreading the Light of Hypnosis and the 2001 Ormond McGill Award.*

Chapter 50
Light Touch Hypnotism

Instrumental in bringing this method to the public was fellow hypnosis instructor Walter Salas, who, having had a headache for five days "that just wouldn't quit," accepted my offer of the "light touch method" that I developed in the early 70s for a psychic arts research group to relieve headaches and back pain. I told Walt that after I had previously demonstrated it on Joseph Goodman, MD, head of the Acupuncture Society of Great Britain, Joe said, "Your light touch method creates astounding, relaxing sensations, stimulating the pilo-motor nerves to the brain stem and skin, to cause a contraction of the small, smooth muscle groups at the base of each hair in that area, causing it to stand up; creating a massive array of "Goose Bumps!"

Impressed at how well it worked, Walt began using light touch hypnotism on clients. It was so successful he asked me to demonstrate the method to the National Guild of Hypnotists, and exclaimed, "Connie, this method needs to be shared with the world!"

Mini Explanation

The subject is seated on a backless stool, spine erect, head well balanced, shoulders and arms relaxed, elbows accessible to touch.

Beginning just below the waist, from the spine out, place the backside of your fingernails on both sides of the spine and around to imaginary side seams under the armpit. Not to any erogenous zones!

Applying light pressure, have client close their eyes and describe out loud while visualizing a special place with fresh, healthy, cleansing, healing air, breathing deeply, a natural, healthy breathing all the while you are performing the procedure. Proceed with calm patter about "continuing to breathe healthy healing air while relaxing," moving slowly up and outward, forming a pattern of vertical "Vs" up to the neck.

Change directions from the base of the skull down to form a series of horizontal figure eights, covering the width of the shoulders, spine, and back, down to just below the waist.

Reverse and re-trace the pattern back up, including arms, using figure eights up to the base of the skull. Complete with hands on shoulders, thumbs lightly stroking only upward to the occipital area. When finished, have the client open his eyes and lead him by his shoulders to a recliner and complete the session as you would normally. It is non-invasive.

This method releases the endorphins needed to reduce and stifle pain, encourage better circulation to alleviate painful symptoms of Raynauds, fibromyalgia, headache, and back pain, including stomach stress from chemotherapy.

It arouses and reprograms genetically one's internal mechanism in the brain, producing a massive sensation of goose bumps without drugs.

Kinesthetically triggering that large area of nerves, it overwhelms the sensory system, stimulating the brain stem and cortex in a disproportionate measure.

Goose bumps change or recharge the electrical activity in one's brain, spontaneously releasing pain-reducing endorphins.

Arrector Pili

A smooth muscle of the skin, attached to a hair follicle, extends upward on a slant and reacts to touch stimuli. When contracted, the muscle pulls the hair erect, thus "goose bumps."

Constance G. Palinsky, is a National Guild of Hypnotists Certified Advanced Clinical Hypnotherapy Instructor, hypnotherapist, artist and writer. Intrigued, she studied extensively, and has been involved in scientific and therapeutic hypnosis for 57 years. Professionally, since 1974, she wrote and performed EEG research on hypnosis and the effects of wrong words on humans. She is 82, and resides in Florida.
Received First Hypnosis Research Award ~ National Guild of Hypnotists ~1990

www.ingramcontent.com/pod-product-compliance
Lightning Source LLC
LaVergne TN
LVHW091009080826
845145LV00003B/1188

* 9 7 8 1 8 8 5 8 4 6 0 6 8 *